The Doctor's Luck

THE DOCTOR'S LUCK

To: Becky, Love & Best Wishes

Nancy Glenn Powell

NANCY GLENN POWELL

Dedicated

To David Powell, my husband and friend.

And to Evelyn Brown, my editor and friend.

CONTENTS

The Doctor's Luck

1 ~ Unwelcome Gift

An old farmer turns toward Doctor Tom before leaving the office. "Doc, I left two young roosters, good for frying, in a crate beside your house. I'll pick up my crate tomorrow. This depression has left me without money to pay, but I hope those are enough. Although, if you like, I'll wring their necks and skin them before I go."

"Yes, that will be nice. I'll get Rita to fry them for dinner, but I wouldn't ask her to kill them, and I won't have time. I'll get you a pan for the meat."

After handing a pan to the farmer, the doctor steps to the window. "Rita, did you notice Betty Ann when you came to work? She's sitting in that swing."

"No. I don't guess I looked that way." Rita, Doctor Tom's housekeeper, turns to stare at the teenage girl whose head droops toward the ground, her curly hair a tangled mess, and her dress wrinkled and dirty.

"Her daddy brought her in yesterday and asked me to perform an abortion. I refused, and told him saving lives is my job."

He shakes his head and sits at the table. "She's only fourteen and has the mind of a three or four-year-old. Her daddy said he saw a young man leaving the house one day when he came in from plowing. He found Betty Ann hiding under her bed, crying, but by then, the boy was nowhere in sight."

He stands to look out the window again. "After a few of my questions, Betty's dad told me his wife left them years ago after the child fell off a ladder and hit her head." He stares into his cup.

"She was almost four when she fell—a normal healthy child until the accident. Now, to the best of my knowledge, she is almost seven months pregnant, and I heard two hearts beating, although I didn't tell him. He was panicked about taking care of Betty and one baby."

"That's sad, but why did he leave her here?"

Doctor Tom lifts the cup of coffee and takes a sip. "I'm hoping Betty's pa had business in town and will come back later. He was upset that I wouldn't get rid of her baby and said she is more than he can take care of and work. I sympathize. He's right. She can't raise one baby, certainly not two, but I won't do an abortion and destroy two healthy lives—nor one. The babies won't inherit her problem."

Staring into his cup, Doctor Tom shakes his head before speaking in a slow, soft tone. "Rita, the doctor I bought this place from, kept a file on every one of his patients. Last evening, I found the one for Betty's mama; it stated she was a devoted mother, and almost went crazy after Betty's accident. The woman told Doctor John that every time she looked at Betty, she wanted to cry and felt a horrible feeling of shame for not seeing the child before the ladder tipped over. She thought about killing herself but didn't have the courage. The file notation said Betty's pa didn't miss a day without telling her the accident was her fault.

"When she couldn't take his accusations anymore, she left. There's a newspaper article in the file dated a few days later. It tells of a woman killed. Witnesses said she walked onto the railroad tracks and stood there with her hands folded, singing a lullaby until the train hit her. That woman was Betty's mama."

Rita wrings her hands. "Oh, the poor woman. It's impossible to watch a child every minute. More than once, when my Ben was around three or four, I lifted him off the ladder, going to my barn loft."

"I didn't like that man the minute he pushed Betty into my office with tears streaming down her face. After reading Doctor John's file, I blame Betty's pa for his wife's death. He loaded more guilt onto her broken heart than the poor woman could take."

Rita jumps at a loud knock on the kitchen door. Rushing to take a pan of chicken from the old farmer, she thanks him, sets the chicken on the counter and pours cold water over it. "What do you want me to do with this meat?"

He takes another sip of coffee, swallows, and breathes deep. "Fry it and cook some of these vegetables sitting around to go with it. If your boys come by, tell them to stay for the meal. We can't eat two chickens. Most of the people around here pay with vegetables, eggs, or chicken; consequently, I can't pay you. Can you and your boys survive on some of this food until someone pays with money?"

"I- I need enough cash to buy dress material. My work dress is coming apart. I had to wear my Sunday dress today."

With a sigh, his shoulders slump. "I hate to ask you to wait, but I can't give you what I don't have. There's a trunk in the second bedroom; it belonged to my mother and sister. The railroad sent it to me months after the funeral. It's full of their things—none of the contents were damaged in the train wreck. Look in it and see if you can fix any of those dresses to fit you. My sister was about your size. You can have the trunk and everything inside."

"Are you sure you want to give them away?"

He nods, "Yes. I can't wear them. Mama wouldn't want me to store them to rot with old age."

A knock vibrates the front door. Doctor Tom gulps the last of his coffee and goes to greet a patient.

Rita rushes to open the trunk. It is full of attractive clothes, but most are for a much heavier woman. Finding a cotton dress printed with tiny green leaves, she locks the door, slips out of her navy blue, and into the green print. It fits. Sorting through the others, she finds two more cotton dresses that she can wear for work. With her white smock buttoned over the green print, she returns to the kitchen. Only a few wrinkles show.

She washes dirty dishes left in the sink, before cutting up the chicken and getting it ready to fry. She puts dried pinto beans in water to soak for supper, peels potatoes and leaves them setting in cold water until closer to lunchtime, cuts up cabbage, and makes a pan of biscuits that she covers with a clean dishtowel. Next, she mixes sugar cookies, cuts them into star shapes, and places them on a large metal pan to bake in the kerosene stove. Doctor Tom likes to have fresh cookies every day to share with children visiting his office—and to feed his own sweet tooth.

Glancing through the window to check on Betty Ann, she sees the girl in the same spot—not moving the swing. Her cheeks are wet with tears, but she makes no sound. The sun has risen hot, and she is no longer in the shade.

Rita takes a pan of cookies from the oven, slides another in to bake, and goes out the back door. "Betty Ann, come in the house with me for a cool drink and a cookie."

The girl jumps at the sound of her name and looks frightened.

"Come on inside, where it's cooler. I made sugar cookies. Do you want one?"

In slow motion, the blond head nods, but the girl does not otherwise move or speak until Rita smiles and holds out her hand.

"Daddy gone. He say Doctor Tom take care of me. Mama not want me. Daddy not want me."

Rita steps close and takes her hand. "Come with me. I'll give you a cookie and some cold milk. We like cookies, don't we?"

Betty Ann nods, follows Rita into the house, and smiles when she sees the pan of warm cookies.

Rita hands her a wet washcloth. "Wash your hands and face. Then you can have the four cookies on this plate, and I'll get you a glass of milk from a jar in the ice-box." The milk is another payment for a doctor's visit.

"I have to fix lunch while you eat your cookies."

Between answering the door and registering patients for the doctor, Rita cooks the noon meal and keeps Betty entertained in the kitchen with a rag doll from the toy box kept for young patients. She is not sure how much Betty understands, but as long as Rita is talking, the girl sits staring and seems to listen. Keeping her voice low so as not to disturb patients in the waiting room, Rita continues.

After Doctor Tom gives thanks for lunch and all blessings, Rita sets a plate in front of Betty. It contains a chicken leg, mashed potatoes covered with gravy, a biscuit, and stewed cabbage.

Betty gobbles every bite, pushes her plate away, and stares at Doctor Tom. "Daddy gone. He say Doctor Tom take care of me. Daddy not want me. Betty bad."

The doctor's eyes open wide as he realizes her pa has not returned to pick her up and may never return. "Where did your daddy go?"

She shrugs and slings an arm in the air. "Away. Far away. Never come back. I stay with you."

He takes another deep breath and turns to Rita. "Every day, my life seems to complicate itself. As soon as you cover this food, I'd like you to walk over to the sheriff's home and, if he's there, explain this to him, but don't mention the pregnancy or the requested abortion. Ask him to come by around four-thirty."

Doctor Tom hands Betty another cookie and takes one for himself as Rita puts all the leftovers in glass-covered dishes. He has such a sad look on his face that Rita wonders if he might cry. She has never seen a man cry and is sure her pa would have fought to his death before letting anyone see him shed tears.

The sheriff tells Rita the orphanage is full and cannot take another child, but he'll go out to Betty's pa's farm to see if the man left the area, and he'll ask people around town and try to find someone to take Betty if her papa is gone.

Rita is glad that Betty is rocking a doll on the back porch when the sheriff steps into the waiting room—perhaps, the child cannot hear the men through the building—still, Rita clenches her teeth as the sheriff's loud voice seems to reverberate. She is not sure how much of the men's conversation Betty could understand but does not want her to hear it.

"Doc, there's not an animal left on that man's farm, and everything is closed up tighter than a jug. I checked around town for volunteers to help, but not a soul is willing to take a full-grown girl with the mind of a three-year-old."

The doctor's face wrinkles into a frown; "Sheriff, you know, I can't keep her. A man alone can't keep a full-grown girl that's not blood kin. Imagine the talk that would travel throughout the county."

The sheriff's eyebrows go up, and he props an elbow on the chair arm covering his mouth with fingers as he shakes his head. "I don't know what to tell you."

"Sheriff, if I knew you were grinning behind your hand, I'd kick that chair out from under you. I tell you, I can't keep the girl. What could I do when I have to make a house call? Doesn't the state pay the orphanage so much for each child they keep? Maybe you can set it up for the state to pay some widow to keep her."

"It takes months to get state money approved for anything."

"What about the mental hospital?"

"Have you ever been to that place? I wouldn't send an animal there."

"Sheriff, you have to help me. Her pa dumped her in my yard and left."

"Well, I can't take her. I don't have a woman to look after a girl. What could I do with her when I have to hunt a criminal?"

"You can lock her in jail. That's better than leaving her alone in my house while I'm gone for hours helping sick folk. Imagine the mess I would have. She'd have the house burned down within a week."

After an hour of arguing, the sheriff walks away without offering a rational solution.

Doctor Tom insists on Rita and her boys staying in his home until he finds a solution to his problem. She only agrees to stay Friday and Saturday nights. "On Sunday, I'll have to go home to water my garden and wash the boys' clothes."

Rita resolves to stay the two nights as promised. The first night Betty sleeps in a double bed with Rita. The girl kicks, talks in her sleep and flops from side to side. Rita wakes more tired than when she went to bed. The second night, Doctor Tom finds Betty a cot.

Sunday morning, Doctor Tom takes Betty to the local church building, sits her on the first row, and stands in front of the congregation explaining what has happened. He states that some good Christian woman needs to take the child.

One outspoken woman stands and says she already has a child and can't handle another, but Doctor Tom should pick himself a wife among the widows of the community.

The doctor jumps to his feet, yelling, "I can't afford a wife, and I don't want a wife." He almost runs from the church.

Rita wants to follow and help Betty and Doctor Tom, but her boys are eager to get home, fish, and swim in the creek, and she needs to do laundry.

Rita watched with compassion while Dr. Tom made his speech in front of the congregation. With pure force, she held her emotions inside when he rushed from the building.

Betty Ann sat on the bench, looking confused as men, women, and children passed. One man reached out to pat her shoulder, but Betty jerked away as if he was going to beat her. Only the preacher and the sheriff remained with Betty when Rita and her boys left the churchyard.

The Doctor's Luck

2 ~ A Stranger in the Barn

Walking home with her boys, Rita tells them, "I would take Betty, but sometimes we don't know from where our next meal will come. I can't take in another mouth to feed."

Ben and George look at her with frowns, and Ben says. "Mama, she's wild. You couldn't take care of her every day. She outweighs you by almost fifty pounds. If she wanted to, she could kill you with her bare hands."

Rita smiles at them. "Boys, she's a baby in a big girl's body."

"Mama, don't think about taking her. I'll leave if you do."

Looking at Ben, her youngest, Rita scowls. "Oh, son, don't be teasing me. You know I can't take care of her and work. I love you two boys more than anything in this world, but I feel sorry for that child. She has no one to love her."

George kicks a pebble from the road. "There's a reason no one loves her. She's mean. She bit Ben, and pulled my hair when I tried to make her turn loose."

Sunday afternoon, while Rita scrubs stains from the boy's overalls, her thoughts drift back to when she was near Betty's age—innocent and naïve. *I had no idea what was happening when Luke grabbed me. He held me so tight I couldn't get free—with his hand clamped over my mouth, I couldn't even breathe.* Taking a deep breath, she pauses to look toward the creek before continuing to remember. Her recollection is not happy.

I didn't have a mama to tell me about things a teenage girl should know. Weeks later, Daddy realized my condition. He talked to the preacher, caught Luke, and made him marry me. Now I'm twenty-six with two boys, no husband, and living on Pa's farm with no way to work it. A rare tear slides down her face. Wiping her cheek on a sleeve, she says, "Thank you Lord for my blessings, and forgive my ungrateful complaints. I have a bounty of reasons to be thankful."

She sloshes a pair of overalls in the rinse tub, flops them over a clothesline wire, straightens the rub-board, and reaches for another pair. Most Christian women would not consider doing a wash on Sunday, but Rita's boys need to be clean while spending time around the doctor's office, and she has to work tomorrow.

After all the clothes are hanging to dry, Rita cooks the pot of beans left soaking before church and mixes a pan of cornbread. Now is a good time to water—shade from a big oak tree is almost covering the garden. The ground will absorb the moisture without steaming the plants. She dips a bucket into the wash water and transfers it to a garden row—that and several buckets from the well leaves the ground around all the plant roots soggy. *Maybe this will keep them alive until it rains, or I get a chance to water again.*

The boys caught four fish, and they cleaned them while Rita gathered in her laundry. Fried crisp, the fish are delicious with juicy beans and cornbread.

After supper, they sit on the narrow front porch enjoying the evening. With millions of stars lighting the sky, they listen to night sounds—a coyote howling far up on the mountain, an owl hooting in the woods, and thousands of chirping crickets in nearby trees. George shuffles his feet and turns his face toward Rita. "Here on the porch, I like hearing the night noises, but to be in the woods alone, they would be mighty scary."

Rita fans her apron and grins. "If you start thinking about them, the things you can't hear are more frightening."

"Do you mean snakes and spiders?"

"Yes, and panthers on the prowl, or evil men."

"Yeah." He pulls his bare feet off the doorstep and onto the porch. "Mama, have you ever shot a gun?"

"Yes, many times. Pa took me hunting when I was a girl. Then, he had a rifle. I used to kill squirrels, rabbits, and I shot two turkeys. Pa cleaned them; I cooked them, and we ate every bite. I didn't shoot something unless I planned to eat it—except a snake. Once I shot a rattler, and I shot a black snake that was eating a baby chicken."

"Really!"

"Yes. It had already eaten two when I heard the hen cackling and ran out with Pa's shotgun."

What happened to Grandpa's rifle?"

"Ah, George. I guess Luke sold it. Anyway, it disappeared."

"I never thought of you as a hunter. Could you shoot a man if one came here to hurt us?"

She clears her throat, and all of a sudden, her voice is harsh. "I would do anything in my power to protect you and Ben."

"But shoot a man?"

"Yes. I wouldn't hesitate to shoot if I knew you were in

danger."

Ben stands and rests his hand on the screen door handle. "Mama, don't you think it's time to go inside for our Bible story?"

"Yes, son. It's getting late."

Once they are inside, Ben closes and locks the wood door.

She picks up her Bible and turns to look at the closed door. "Ben, why don't you hook the screen until time for bed? It's sweltering in here."

He hesitates. "I heard something walking in the woods. I like the door closed."

Her eyebrows go up, but she doesn't comment, as he pulls the curtains together.

Placing the Bible on the table, she turns up the wick on the oil lamp, sits in her rocker beside the table, and opens the book. Each time the rocker squeaks, she notices Ben flinch, and George glance toward the open window. All right, boys, tell me what you heard or seen in the woods. Was it a man?"

They drop their heads for a second before George goes to close the window and wedge a stick over it so no one outside can slide it open. "A man stood in the woods watching us today. We tried to pretend we didn't see him, but he didn't go away. We couldn't tell what he looked like, he had an old floppy hat pulled low over his face, and he stayed in the shadows. We already had four fish, so we gathered our things and came to the house."

"Boys, these days, a lot of people have moved into the woods. People from the cities who can't afford to pay rent have nowhere to go. Sometimes, families with women and children are forced to camp in the woods. Don't worry about it. You two can make a pallet on the floor in my room tonight. I'll keep Pa's shotgun beside my bed. All next week we'll be staying at the doctor's to help with Betty."

"Oh, boy. I dread being around her." George grumbles. "Mama, do you mind if we ask Mr. Smith for a job helping him haul hay? I'd almost work for free to stay away from Betty. She bites and pulls hair."

"You can ask, but don't be too disappointed if he says no. A lot of full-grown men are looking for work."

After she turns out the lamps and crawls into bed with the shotgun leaning against the headboard, her heart is still racing. The idea of someone watching her boys chilled her to the bone, and she can't shake the sensation. Eleven and twelve-year-olds are not old enough to tote guns for hunting and protection unless they have had a good pa training them. She cannot teach them because she has to work. They would be very disappointed if she told them to stay away from the creek. Fishing is not only fun; it gives them a feeling of helping her provide food for the table.

Long after both boys are asleep, she lies awake, restless, and wondering what to do. The room is stifling hot with the windows closed. Dare she open one to allow a breeze inside?

Sliding off the bed, she pulls back a curtain and scans the yard. Walking barefoot through the house, she peeps out every window. From the kitchen, she stares toward the barn. Inside the cow lot, something moves in the moonlight. The dark form of a man disappears into the barn. Most likely, it's someone passing through and needing a place to rest for the night, but she will leave the windows closed.

She closes the curtain, picks up an old newspaper, and fans herself before going to fan the boys on the pallet. For the rest of the night, she slides her hand toward the gun every time an owl hoots, or the wind causes a tree branch to scrape the side of the house.

Rita wakes with Ben calling, "Mama, are you going to work this morning?"

Rolling from the bed, she yells. "Oh no, I forgot to set the alarm. Run to another room to put your clothes on. I've got to get myself dressed for work. I'll fix you some breakfast in the doctor's kitchen."

The date is August 1932. The bank closed without returning the money Rita saved to pay taxes. The following day Luke, her husband, left to look for work. Two years have passed, and she has not heard from him.

Is he dead or rotting in a ditch somewhere far away? Is he too ashamed to admit he can't take care of his family, or is he just being Luke—letting her worry about their boys? Over and over, she asks herself those questions but tells herself that he loved his boys, even though he never said those words to her.

Three dresses, one for work, one for Sunday, and the green print that once belonged to Doctor Tom's sister, hang on wooden hangers over a nail behind the door. Taking down her cotton print, she notices the threadbare spot on the front where she often leans against a file drawer. Her smock would cover the place while working in the doctor's office, but she cannot go to town with her slip showing through the threads. She slides into the green print.

Rushing toward the door, she calls, "Ben, you and George know the chores you have to do. Clean yourselves up when you finish and meet me when I get off work. If I get paid today, I'll need you to carry the groceries home."

Doctor Tom has an early patient in his office when she arrives. She cannot understand their words, but a deep voice lets her know it is a man. Slipping on a white smock, she buttons the front and goes down the hall to the kitchen to make coffee—always her first chore of the day. Doctor Tom likes strong coffee with rich cream. As far as she can tell, coffee is his one and only vice.

Looking around, Rita remembers a conversation she overheard at the grocery store. A man said Doctor Tom bought this big house with its waiting room, patient rooms, and five bedrooms for less than the cost of a small house, but it was only offered to a doctor willing to practice in the community.

Without pondering, she rushes to fry five eggs and make toast instead of the biscuits she often makes. The boys wolf their eggs and leave to talk to Mr. Smith about a hay-hauling job. Betty eats her toast and egg then goes to sit on the porch with a cookie in each hand. The coffee perks for several minutes before the doctor comes from his office.

"I need my coffee. I didn't sleep much last night. Betty must walk in her sleep. I gave her warm milk and cookies three times. I figured she would wet the bed, but she likes the bathroom toilet and ran in there every time she got up."

The doctor has dark circles under his eyes. He drops into a chair as if his body weighs more than he can carry. Taking a cup of hot brew, he sniffs the aroma and takes a sip. "Rita, you make the best coffee I've ever tasted."

"Thank you, sir."

With a sigh, he asks, "Will you watch Betty while I take a nap?"

She nods. "Of course."

"Wake me if you see anyone coming toward the door, and make another pot of coffee in an hour. I'll need help to stay on my feet today."

The next patient arrives within twenty minutes, and the morning drags with lots of problems for the doctor. Rita makes fresh coffee every hour—Doctor Tom gulps it and returns to work.

When Doctor Tom sits to eat lunch, Rita pours his coffee and says, "I'm sorry I came in late for work. I didn't sleep well last night, and I overslept this morning."

He waves his hand in the air, "Forget it." He picks up his coffee and a sandwich. "Come to the porch while Betty finishes her food. I need to talk, and I need someone to listen—someone who won't laugh."

3 ~ Betty's Bath

The doctor eases into a chair and smiles a weak smile. "Yesterday, when I left the church building, I didn't stop until I was home behind locked doors. I pulled every window shade and sat trembling with pent-up anger beside a lamp to read, but near dark, I looked out the kitchen window. There on the swing sat Betty Ann, tears drizzling down her cheeks, and my heart melted.

"From the porch, I motioned to her and called, 'Betty Ann, come inside for a glass of cold milk and some cookies.'

"While she ate cookies and drank milk, I ran the bathtub half full and dumped a few soap flakes in the water. I hung one of Mama's dresses on a hook behind the door, placed an undergarment and a towel on the toilet seat, and called to her. 'Betty put the last of your cookie in your mouth and take a bath in the bubbles I made for you.'

"She shook her head. 'I not like bath.'

"I told her, 'You are starting to smell like a sweaty horse. You have to bathe. You can close the door, but I want you to scrub every spot on your body with the washcloth. Later, we'll wash your hair in the sink.'

"She yelled, 'I not like bath!' She jumped up and started toward the door. I grabbed her arm, led her into the bathroom, and told her, 'Kick off your shoes. You have to get in the tub.' Before I could say more, she stepped in the tub with her shoes and clothes on.

"Sit down," I demanded.

"With a splash, she dropped in the tub. Water and bubbles covered the floor and my shoes. As if God was standing in the room, I said, Lord, if no one else will help me, I'll have to do this. Help me—please. Please!

"I unbuttoned Betty's dress, pulled it over her head, and began to wash her back with the cloth. The rusty coating on her skin rolled off as I scrubbed. It was evident that she had not taken a real bath in months. She sat still, her face puckered into a frown until I gave her the cloth and told her to wash her face.

"Giggling, she dipped the cloth in the bubbles and scrubbed at her face, chest, and stomach.

"She continued to giggle but followed my instructions until she had washed her entire body, except her hair.

"I wanted to dunk her head and soap her dirty hair but thought that might frighten her more than I wanted to deal with so late in the day. Instead, I pulled the plug to drain the water. When it made a loud slurping noise, Betty rolled over the side of the tub, plopping onto the floor, her eyes wide with fear.

"I tossed a towel around her shoulders, dropped another on the floor, and told her to stand on it. She began to slip before getting her feet on the towel, but before I could grab her, she stood giggling—a giant baby in a blanket." He shakes his head.

"I told her to go in the bedroom while I cleaned up the water, to dry herself, put on the dress, and the clean underpants I gave her.

"Her complaining got louder and louder as I mopped water. 'Can't! Can't do it. Betty, too fat,' she yelled.

"Tossing the sopping towels in the tub, I went to see if I could help her. She had one foot in the dress sleeve and was trying to pull it up her leg.

"Betty, sit on the bed and let me help," I said.

"She plopped down on the bed, letting her feet and the dress dangle toward the floor.

"I reached for the dress, tugging as I talked to God. 'Lord, why did you give me this challenge? Is it not enough that I have needy patients with no money to pay? Lord, I need help. The grocer wants money, Rita needs money, and the pharmacy is threatening to cut off my medical supplies. In Jesus' name, I pray—I plead, Lord—please help me. I'm sure the Lord must have intervened because a little more stress and I would have gone over the edge. While I was about to have a breakdown, Betty kept kicking and giggling. One pudgy foot hit me in the stomach, taking away my breath. The dress settled to the floor as she kicked the air, naked, and happy. At last, recovering my breath, I grabbed the underwear, held one leg open, and with a gruff voice, demanded, 'Betty put your foot in here.'

"Sliding closer to the edge of the bed, she put one foot in, and then the other. She slid off the mattress and pulled up the pair of Mama's big underpants. I dropped the dress over her head, directed a hand into each sleeve, and buttoned the front. Mama was a plump woman, so the dress had ample room around Betty's expanding middle.

"She stood, swaying from side to side. 'Pretty dress. Betty pretty.'

"Stepping away, I had to smile. Yes. Yes, very pretty, but we need to brush your hair.

"She yelled, 'No! No! Hair hurt.'

"The dress sash was crumpled on the floor. I picked it up, showed it to Betty, and said, 'Let me brush your curls, a little bit, and I'll put this pretty ribbon in your hair.'

"She frowned and hugged herself, but didn't scream as I rubbed the brush over her head. After a few swipes, not removing all the tangles, I tied the sash around her head with a bow on top. The streamers hung down her back, and I offered her a hand mirror so she could look at herself.

"Nodding, she repeated, 'Pretty. Pretty.'"

With a heavy sigh, he takes a sip of the coffee that is getting cold. "Rita, what am I going to do? I can't turn her out in the street. When I wasn't awake checking on her safety, I was praying for God's help." He sighs and shakes his head. "I'll be dead within a year if I have to maintain this pace, and I haven't even tried to wash her hair."

"I'll help you. My boys and I will stay here during the week and go home on the weekends to water and do chores. This afternoon, I'll do my best to wash her hair."

"Thank you. Maybe Betty will calm down after a while, and we can deal with whatever comes next."

Rita takes a deep breath. "I don't mind helping. I'm glad to do anything I can, but I hope the town gossips don't start a vulgar story about me staying here."

"Oh, don't worry about that. I'm the town doctor, and you are a respectable member of the church. Besides, your boys will be here every night."

After lunch, with the dishes washed and the food put away, Rita warms a pan of water and brings a bottle of shampoo from the bathroom to the kitchen. Betty asks for cookies, but Rita tells her that she can have four cookies after she gets her hair washed.

"No! Hair wash hurt."

"Your head has dirt on it. If we don't wash it, bugs will start crawling in your hair, and they'll bite. I'll put shampoo bubbles on your head and be very gentle. Bugs don't like shampoo, so they'll go down the drain."

"Betty, not like hair wash. Betty, not like bugs." She shakes her head hard as if trying to shake out bugs.

"It won't hurt if you'll bend over the pan of warm water and let me rub your hair. When I rinse out the bubbles, your hair will be pretty and smell pretty."

Betty frowns, but walks to the sink and dunks the top of her head in the pan of warm water.

Rita dumps a handful of shampoo on Betty's head and gently rubs it through her hair and onto her scalp as she sings, *Mary had a Little Lamb*. At the end of the first verse, Rita adds, *And Betty's hair will be clean like Mary's Lamb, Mary's Lamb. Her hair will be clean as snow.*

Betty giggles and says, "Clean like Mary's Lamb."

Betty, singing with Rita, lifts her head from the pan and screams as suds run across her face and into her eyes. "Hurt. Eye hurt." She grabs her dress tail to rub her eyes.

Tossing a towel over Betty's head, Rita tries to stop the fountain of water streaming onto the kitchen floor. "Betty, lean over the sink so I can rinse your hair. You've got shampoo in your eye. Touch it with this towel."

When Betty stops screaming, and the doctor's patients go back to their seats away from the kitchen door, Rita rinses Betty's hair twice and rubs a cream conditioner through it. Rita pats Betty's hair with a soft towel and lets Betty brush it as Rita holds a mirror.

Putting the brush on the table, Betty takes the mirror in one hand and a cookie in another, and stares at herself, smiling. "No bugs. Betty's hair clean. Bugs go down drain."

She giggles when Doctor Tom comes into the kitchen and asks, "Who is this girl with the beautiful clean hair?"

He laughs and steps back. "And why is the floor, and my nurse all wet?"

4 ~ The Mockingbird

The following morning, Betty whines to go outside. Rita tells her, "You can play outside, but stay under the tree with the swing where I can see you from the window."

"Okay. I stay under tree."

Rita is washing dishes when she hears screaming. Looking through the window, she sees Betty on the ground with a mocking bird hovering over her, making almost as much noise.

She rushes to the yard where Betty is holding a bird's nest over her head and squeezing a baby bird with the other hand. "Give me the nest. Turn loose. This belongs to that mama bird."

Betty drops the crumpled mass of twigs, and the limp bird that she has squeezed to death. Rita tosses the bird's nest into a bush and encourages the screaming girl to stand.

A skinny little woman crosses the road and approaches Rita. "You need to watch her closer. She climbed into that tree and dumped those poor birds on the ground. It's a wonder the mama didn't peck her eyes out. I hope it nipped her enough that she'll remember the pain before tearing down another nest."

Without a word, Rita leads Betty into the house, sets her on a chair, and washes her hands and face. "Show me the bird bite."

Betty lifts a hand with a red scratch and a peck mark. Rita swabs iodine across the wounds causing Betty to scream again.

"You better sit on the floor and play with your doll. The big bird might bite you again if you go outside."

Betty holds up her injured hand. "Bad bird bite me."

With her rag doll in one hand, Betty leans against the kitchen wall, licks the salt from a saltine cracker, and mumbles about the mean bird.

The waiting room door remains half-way open, so Rita can see and go to greet the patients coming in. Two men waiting to see the doctor heard Betty's commotion and sit laughing. One says, "I don't envy Doctor Tom or his housekeeper. They have their hands full. I'd pack a bag and move away if someone dropped a problem like her on my doorstep."

Betty tries to help Rita shell a basket of peas left by a patient. After Betty breaks several and spills her pan, Rita tells her that she has helped enough and to rock the doll because it is about to cry. Sitting in a rocker, pulled into the kitchen from a bedroom, Betty talks to her toy until she falls asleep, and it slips to the floor. Rita is relieved and continues to shell peas until the doctor comes to the kitchen for a drink of water.

"Rita, wake her. Keep her awake all day, or we won't get any sleep tonight."

Washing her face with cold water wakes Betty, but she is not happy. She pushes the cloth away and kicks her feet. At last, she calms down when Rita tells her she can help make cookies.

Rita mixes the dough, but instead of using a dough roller, she lets Betty flour her hands and roll out little balls. Betty forms one and eats the second. The third she puts in her pocket.

"Betty, you can't save them in your pocket. A mouse will crawl in your pocket and eat the cookie tonight while you sleep. We have to put them on the pan and cook them."

"A mouse!" She giggles, puts the dough ball on the pan and makes another. She rolls them fast. Some are tiny, some are big, and some are uneven blobs.

Rita works fast to rush the chore and helps Betty to mash them flat with her hand, sighing with relief when the last pan is ready for the oven.

With the cookies baking, Rita mixes a pan of cornbread, cuts cabbage to boil, and adds more water to the peas she put on earlier.

"What you do now?" Betty asks.

"I have to slice some ham and fry it."

"I help." Betty smiles and reaches for a knife on the counter.

"No. Put the knife down. We have to wash our hands, and then I'll cut, and you can put it in the pan."

"No-o-o." "I cut."

"Little girls don't use knives. You might cut your finger and get blood on the meat. You can put the meat in the pan."

"Okay." She pouts her lips and sits in a chair, frowning with folded arms."

Rita's patience is wearing thin. Glancing at Betty, she whispers a prayer. "Lord, please be with me. I need to help the doctor so he can sleep. I promised I'd stay, but I'll need to go home tonight. I may start screaming if I have to remain with Betty for more than ten hours but, with your help, I'll try my best to keep calm."

Hours past noon, the boys rush in, both talking at once, telling Rita Mr. Smith gave them jobs of hauling hay.

"S-h-e-e-e. Be quiet. Doctor Tom has patients. Talk one at a time. You first, George."

"Mr. Smith hired us, but he said we'll have to split the wage that he would pay a full-grown man. He was sharpening the blades on his mowing machine as he told us he planned to cut this afternoon, rake tomorrow, and we can haul the loose hay to his barn on Wednesday afternoon. His wife came outside and insisted we stay and eat with them. We had a feast."

She frowns. "Will Mr. Smith help you, or will you be driving the team with the wagon?"

They shrug. "We don't know, but we have to learn to farm sometime. Mr. Smith wanted us to ask you if he can cut the hay off our farm. He said it's been such a dry year, and hay is scarce."

She nods. "It will be good to have our hay cut. We don't have animals to eat it. I've been worried about a fire starting in those dry fields and burning everything."

Ben raises his foot. "Look, Mama. He said we couldn't haul hay with bare feet, because the hayfield has briars and stumps that could ruin a foot. He told us his wife saved all the shoes, boots, and clothes that belonged to their son when he was growing up. He laughed and said his wife wouldn't throw anything away because someone might need it."

Rita smiles. "Those are nice boots, and he gave you both a pair? You can wear those to school this winter. I've been praying for God to see your needs."

George taps her arm, "His wife gave us each a bag of clothes, shirts, overalls and blue jeans. I hope some of them fit—my boots are a little too big, but my feet are still growing, and I can wear thick socks when the weather turns cold."

"Yes. I hope some of the clothes fit. School will start soon."

Betty scoots from her chair and wraps her arms around Ben. He struggles to unwind himself and runs out the door.

"George, wash your hands and help me set the table for supper. Doctor Tom is with his last patient." They rush to get the food on the table and get Betty in her chair before the doctor comes in. Ben stands behind the screen door until after the blessing, then he slips inside and sits next to George.

Betty grabs a piece of ham with her fingers and pokes it in her mouth. She chews with her mouth open until the doctor tells her to close her mouth like George and Ben. She glares at him and spits the meat onto her plate.

Ben eats fast and scurries away from the table.

Doctor Tom takes a silver half dollar from his pocket and holds it toward George. "I'll give this to you boys if you'll take Betty out to the swing and swing her until I finish my meal."

The boys' faces light up with big grins. "Sure thing, Doctor Tom." George reaches for Betty's hand. "Come on, Betty. Let's go swing."

The doctor frowns when Betty lets the door slam. "I've got a terrible headache today. That was all the cash I had—pay for lancing a boil on a sweaty old man's backside, but it's worth the cost for a few minutes of quiet. Besides, I need to talk to you while the children are outside."

Rita catches her breath. "If it's about my wages, don't worry. As long as you don't mind sharing your food, the boys and I are making out fine."

He lowers his head. "Rita, an old doctor in Conway, is planning to retire and has offered to sell his business to me at a reasonable price. I'm thinking about it, but if I go, I want you and your boys to move there too. I believe the people in a bigger town will pay with cash for their doctor visits, and then I'll be able to pay you each week."

"I'll talk to my boys, we'll think it over and let you know tomorrow."

He nods. "Okay. I hope you decide to go. I've enjoyed working with you, and I like your boys. This little town is taking advantage of us. Instead of paying for my services, people give me vegetables, eggs, and chickens. I know some of the old folks and the widows are doing their best, but others, who have money, pay me with items they don't need so they can save their money. Betty's lived here all her life, then a few weeks after I move in, she's dumped in my yard, and not one of the so-called Christians has offered to help with money or their time. If I move to Conway, I'm going to leave her at the sheriff's house and drive away."

"I understand. We could manage if the town's people helped a few hours a day, or a few nights each week. I feel sorry for her, but she wears on a person mentally and physically. No one can tolerate such stress twenty-four hours a day, forever."

"After last night, I'm ready to walk away. People are laughing about our situation, but I don't think it will be funny when they have to ride in a wagon or buggy for almost half a day, rain or shine, sleet or snow, to see a doctor."

"I agree."

He leans forward with his face in his hands. "I'm willing to help with Betty, but I can't do it around the clock for the rest of my life."

Rita nods. "I didn't sleep much last night either. My boys told me they saw a man watching them from the woods, while they were at the creek fishing. Last night, after the boys were asleep, I noticed a man walk into our barn. I don't like the idea of someone watching them and hanging around my farm."

"I don't blame you. Tell the boys to stay in town this week. I'll ask the sheriff to go to your farm and look around."

"Thank you. It was maybe a homeless person passing through and needing a hayloft to rest in, but I propped my daddy's old shotgun at the head of my bed. I didn't open the windows, although it was dreadfully hot last night. I figured it an easy task for a man to pry off a screen, or slit one with a sharp knife."

"Do you think it might have been your husband watching?"

"No. I don't think so. Luke was never a timid fellow. He would have walked right up, acting as if he'd left the day before."

She takes a deep breath and lowers her head to trace a square on the tablecloth with her finger. "If the boys and I move to Conway, I want to talk to a lawyer about getting a divorce from Luke and acquiring custody of my boys. If I don't get legal custody, he might take them away to spite me."

"Do you still love him?"

She huffs a loud sigh and shakes her head. "At fourteen, I liked him for a short while, but I never loved him. He was selfish and forceful—pushing, slapping me, or twisting my arms. He never loved me, but I thought he loved our boys. At least, I wanted them to be loved."

"Move to Conway and work for me. I'll help you get a divorce so you can move on with your life."

"I appreciate your kindness, but I have to talk to my boys before I give you an answer. I want to go. There's no future for me here if you move away." Rita lifts her head to look at his face. "Are you going to the town meeting tonight? People might pitch in to help if they knew they were going to lose their doctor."

"No." His brow furrows. "At this point, I'm disgusted with the town. Most of them are a bunch of selfish people. Although, I'm going to get the sheriff to go to your place and look around. I'll go talk to him now before someone comes in with pain or a complaint."

The doctor grabs his hat from a rack on the wall and walks out the front door into the late afternoon sun.

Rita hears Betty scream. Running through the kitchen, she sees the boys leading the shrieking girl toward the house. Blood pours from Betty's nose.

George's face shows sympathy. "Mama, she wanted to swing high, but she turned loose and fell forward on her face before it got even a little bit high."

"Set her on the porch. Ben, get a cold, wet washcloth. Betty, don't cry. You'll be fine when we wash your face."

"Mama, I told her to hold on, and she said, 'I hold on. Go high.' But she turned loose."

"I believe you, son. She's a three-year-old baby in a big girl's body. We have to remember that." Rita puts her arm around Betty and gently dabs at her skinned nose.

"You're all right now, sweetie. We'll get some cookies, and you'll feel better."

Betty sniffs and pulls the tail of her dress up to wipe her nose. "Cookies. No medicine. Medicine hurt."

"Okay, no medicine."

Rita washes Betty's hands and tells the boys to go wash and bring six cookies from the kitchen."

Ben takes a bite. "Yum-m. These are good."

Betty smiles, tears still streaking her cheeks. "I make cookies."

After eating one, she leans against Rita's arm. Her eyes flicker and close.

"No, Betty. You have to stay awake until bedtime, so you'll sleep tonight." She rewashes the frowning face, but it is no use. Betty's eyes keep closing.

"Boys, I bet she turned loose because she fell asleep from the rocking motion of the swing."

They look at each other and grin. "Then, it's not our fault."

"No, but remember never to push her high. You can't trust a

baby to hold tight. Now, help me get her in the house. I'm going to put her to bed."

Betty snuggles with the ragdoll and goes to sleep.

Rita sits with a dishpan in her lap to shell the remaining peas as her boys rush out the door, telling her they are going to watch Mr. Smith cut his hay.

"Okay, boys, but don't go in his field. Those blades could cripple you for life if you get in front of the mowing machine. Be home in plenty of time before dark."

Doctor Tom comes dragging in the door, looking as if he can barely put one foot in front of the other. "Any patients while I was gone?"

"Not this time. My boys and I will be here all night to watch Betty, so why don't you go on to bed? I can tell from your eyes that you need more rest. I couldn't keep Betty awake. She went to sleep, fell out of the swing, and dozed off against my shoulder while she was eating a cookie." Rita shakes her head. "I put her to bed, so she wouldn't fall and hurt herself more."

"Thanks, Rita. I'll do that. Maybe, with a little more sleep, I can get rid of this headache."

5 ~ Hauling Hay

The following morning Doctor Tom says, "I still have a headache from loss of sleep, worry over Betty, and the decision of moving to Conway, but it's not as bad as yesterday."

Rita pours him a cup of coffee and sets cream and sugar beside it. "Why don't you go back to bed for a while longer? You don't have an appointment until two-thirty. Mrs. Parker is coming then for her checkup. Unless it's an emergency, I'll tell everyone else to come back after three. Tuesday is the slowest day of the week."

"This is Ruth Parker's seventh month. She never made it this far before." He blinks and rubs a hand across his forehead. "I believe I will go to bed for a while. Thank you. Yes, I'll do that. A little more rest should help."

The doctor has closed his bedroom door when the grocer's young son rushes in with his hand bleeding into a flour-sack towel.

"George, you and Ben take Betty into the yard to play while I help this young man."

Rita washes his hand with soapy water, checks the depth of the cut, and applies an antiseptic before bandaging it. "Your cut is shallow and has stopped bleeding, so you don't need stitches. If it starts bleeding again, put a new bandage on it, or you can come back after three when the doctor is in the office."

"Thank you. I think it will be fine. At first, it bled so much that I thought it must be cut deep."

The grocer's son is leaving when a young mother comes in with her two-year-old child. She looks around the office to make sure no one can hear her and whispers close to Rita's ear.

"I don't know how to go about breaking Ellen from wetting her pants. I thought maybe the doctor could tell me. We have an outdoor toilet, and she won't even step inside. She's afraid she'll fall in the hole."

"The doctor will be in his office after three. You can come then if you want, but all little kids are afraid of outdoor toilets. The general store has children's chamber pots. When training my first child, I bought two of them—one for the house and one to leave in the toilet. When you go to the outhouse, insist she sit on her little pot and praise her when she uses it. The second one, inside the house, she can use anytime she has a sudden urge, and remember to praise her for every effort."

"Thank you. I'll try your suggestions."

With the dishpan of peas in her lap, Rita sits in the kitchen. She shells two peas before an older woman steps into the waiting room, leaning on a cane and breathing hard.

Rita looks up. "Hello. May I help you?"

Frowning, the woman says, "Will you call the doctor for me. I have pain in my shoulder. Yesterday, I dug up some roots from my butterfly plant. I keep pieces of it in my chicken's water to prevent chicken cholera, but now I need something for my neck and shoulder."

Rita sets the pan of peas on the table. "He will be in after three, but if you'll step into his office and have a seat, I'll massage your shoulder with ointment."

"That's what he did last time. I'm sure you can do it as well." She hobbles through the office door, unbuttons her dress and pulls it off her shoulder.

Rita finds an ointment with a strong scent of camphor and begins to rub the woman's neck and shoulder.

"The doctor should let you do massages. My pain is about gone."

Rita smiles. "Have you ever tried boiling some of those roots from your butterfly weed and rubbing the mashed root on your sore muscles? My grandma was part Indian, and she used butterfly root and other plants for a lot of ailments for people and animals. I don't know what proportions she used, or if she mixed it with other things, but I remember her saying the roots are poison, so don't use it if you have a cut on your hand."

"My granny used all kinds of roots, berries, and plants for medicine, but I didn't get her to teach me the uses. I would be afraid to try without some instruction."

"I remember a few. My grandma had sacks of plants hanging in the barn loft every winter. Lots of people came to buy them from her."

"Yes, I remember seeing bags of strange plants in our barn loft."

"Mrs. Eller, when you get home, take a towel dipped in hot water, wring it out good, and drape it over your shoulder until it starts to cool. It will relax the muscles, and I think you'll feel much better tomorrow. Also, a cup of chamomile tea before bed will help you relax and sleep better. My grandma drank a cup of that tea every night after her supper."

After a simple lunch for herself and the children, Rita settles in her chair with the dishpan of peas while the boys rush away to Mr. Smith's hayfield.

The waiting room door opens, and Ruth Parker stands for a moment before speaking. "I have an appointment with Dr. Tom at two-thirty." She takes a deep breath. "I'm a little early. Bill dropped me off on his way to work after lunch." She fans the tail of her maternity blouse. "It sure is hot today."

"Yes, it is hot. I think everyone is ready for the cooler days of fall. Come in and sit with me while we wait for the doctor. You can use the rocking chair. I've been all morning trying to get these peas shelled. They belong to Doctor Tom, but I have some late peas planted in my garden. I hope they make before frost."

"We didn't plant a garden this year. I've had morning sickness since day one of this pregnancy. I hope that's a good sign. I was never sick the other times. I've lost three babies before seven months of pregnancy; I guess you know about my grief. I want a baby more than anything, but I think Bill is ready to give up if we lose this one."

"I'll keep you in my prayers. Except for morning sickness, are you feeling well?"

"Yes, until this morning. I'm seven months along, and someone told me Doctor Tom might be moving away."

"I didn't think anyone in town knew about his decision."

"I heard it at the general store. The sheriff told it, and everyone is in a tizzy, above all me. I can't drive to Conway for a doctor."

Rita looks up from the pan of peas. "Can you blame him?" She lowers her voice to a whisper and lowers her head to look under the table where Betty is asleep on a quilt. "That child's pa dropped her off in the yard and left her. She's more work than two tiny babies, and no one from the town has volunteered to help. Her case is so sad. She was normal until almost four years old when she fell off a ladder and hit her head. Since then, her body has grown, but her mind stayed the same."

Ruth shakes her head. "How sad."

"Yes. Doctor Tom asked the church congregation for help and got no results. Another thing, almost no one has paid money for his services. He has a huge stack of bills on his desk and no way to pay the pharmacy, the grocer, the electric company, or the stable for delivering hay and grain for his horse. I haven't received pay for three weeks. These are hard times, and some people cannot pay, but others take advantage by giving him produce they don't need." She shakes her head. "He has a cellar full of cabbage, potatoes, and turnips."

Ruth looks as if she might cry. "I didn't know that was happening."

"Besides worrying about bills, he didn't get to sleep at all on Sunday night, because Betty wouldn't sleep. He asked me to keep her awake without a nap yesterday and today so that she will sleep at night, but I couldn't do it. Last night I put her to bed before sundown. Today I put a quilt on the floor for her to play on with her doll, but she pushed it under the table, crawled on it and fell asleep."

Rita glances at the clock. "Ruth, excuse me a minute. She walks down the hall and taps on the doctor's bedroom door. "Dr. Tom, your two-thirty appointment is here."

With his hair wet and showing comb marks, the doctor appears in the waiting room doorway. "Good afternoon, Ruth. You're looking healthy." The door to his office closes behind them.

Rita bends to wash Betty's face with a cold cloth. "Wake up, Betty. Naptime is over, and a squirrel is in the pecan tree. Let's sit on the porch and watch him. It's cooler on the porch."

Betty sits up, rubbings her eyes. "Does squirrel bite?"

"He would if you catch him, but don't ever try to touch a wild animal. We only want to watch him play in the tree." With her pan of unshelled peas, and a bread pan containing cold leftover popcorn, Rita holds the door open for Betty.

"Betty, you can feed this old popcorn to the squirrel and the birds. It's not good for you to eat. It's stale."

"Not bird. Bird bite."

Betty tosses the popcorn in the yard and turns toward the porch. The mockingbird flies down for a piece, but Betty yells, "No! No!" and waves her arms. The bird flies into a tree and chatters at them.

Soon a squirrel runs out, grabs a grain of corn, and rushes up a tree. Betty giggles and claps her hands. By the time Rita has her peas shelled, there are three squirrels in the yard gathering popcorn. Betty bends over with giggles. Rita is laughing with and at the chubby girl.

"Betty, I need to go wash these peas and put some on to cook.

Do you want to go inside?"

"No. I watch squirrel."

"Those squirrels will bite like the bird if you try to touch one. Stay on the porch. Okay."

"Okay. Bird bite."

Rita washes the peas and has a pan of them ready to cook when she hears a scream and rushes to the porch.

Betty comes stumbling across the yard. "Bird bite me. I not let him eat popcorn. Popcorn for squirrel."

Rita checks Betty's arms and hands. She has a long scratch on one arm.

"Did the bird try to eat the squirrel's corn?"

Betty nods. "I tell bad bird, No."

Rita washes Betty's arm and, before Betty knows what Rita is about to do, wipes iodine over the scratch with a piece of cotton.

Betty screams and flings her arms. "Medicine hurt. No more medicine."

"Okay. No more medicine, but you have to sit in the rocker with your doll and let the medicine dry. If you get down, I'll have to put more medicine on your arm."

She glares at Rita, but nods and begins to rock the doll.

Rita cooks peas, cornbread, cabbage, and fried potatoes for supper while Betty rocks her doll.

The doctor's last patient leaves at six. Rita, Betty, and Doctor Tom sit at the table to eat. Rita knows it is crucial to get all the cut hay in the barn in case they get rain, but she keeps casting worried glances toward the door.

Doctor Tom lifts Betty's arm. "How did she get that scratch?"

"She was in the backyard feeding leftover popcorn to the squirrels but didn't want the mocking bird to get any and tried to shoo it away. She said the bird did it, but I don't know. She might have scratched herself while flinging her arms at the bird; her fingernails are jagged, but she won't let me trim them. I was inside, getting the peas ready to cook, so I'm not sure what happened."

The sun disappears behind the mountain, and crickets chirp in the trees before George and Ben step onto the porch. They are damp and sweat caked with dust. George drops onto the seat of a ladder-back chair where Rita sat earlier shelling peas. With the grace of an older man, Ben lowers himself to sit on the edge of the porch. "Mr. Smith let us haul hay this afternoon. He said with this heat; it dried fast."

White teeth stand out against his tanned face as George grins at Rita. "We're too dirty to come inside. I'll drag the washtub, from the shed, if you'll pour a bucket of water in it. It's dark enough so no one can see us from the street."

"That's a good idea. I'll bring you some soap, towels, and clean clothes."

"Mama, Mr. Smith gave George a silver dollar for our work today. He promised to give us more tomorrow since now we know what to do. Tomorrow, we'll handle the team and wagon by ourselves while he rakes more hay."

"Good, Ben. I'm proud of you and George. Help your brother carry the tub to the porch, while I get you some bathwater. I still have a warm kettle on the stove." She sets two more pans of water on the stove to heat and rushes to get clean clothes from the bag Mrs. Smith gave them the day before.

"Boys, be as quiet as you can. Doctor Tom is trying to get some sleep, and I've already put Betty on the cot in my room."

Rita fills the tub half full of tap water and adds the kettle of warm. "Ben put your clothes in a pile; I'll wash them tomorrow while Betty takes a nap. When you've scrubbed yourself all over, I have warm water on the stove to rinse your soapy hair."

Stepping in the tub, Ben shivers, and whispers, "O-o-h. That kettle didn't warm it much." He scrubs fast. Rita pours warm water over his head and wraps a towel around him.

George says, "I don't need help. Just set the rinse water where I can reach it and put my clothes on the chair. But you can fix me a plate of food. I'm hungry."

Ben devours a plate of food and is reaching for more before George pulls a chair up to the table.

Rita nibbles a cookie and sips a glass of milk while George and Ben finish eating. She doesn't want to rush them and restrains a yawn. She hasn't caught up with the sleep lost on Sunday night while guarding them after they told her about a man watching them at the creek. The good manners taught to her sons do not matter tonight— they are so tired that their left elbows are propped on the table as they operate forks with their right hands. Silently she thanks God for them. *I couldn't stand the grief if something awful happened to my boys. They are my pride and purpose in life.*

The Doctor's Luck

6 ~ The Town's Agreement

Even though Betty took a nap, she sleeps most of the night. However, twice, Rita hears her laughing. Another time, with light through the moonlit window, she sees her flinging her arms and saying, "Bad bird."

George and Ben are up, dressed, and eager to go before Rita has breakfast ready. "Mama, we don't want to be late. Mr. Smith's going to show us how to hitch the horses to the wagon." They grab biscuits from the pan, fill each with a fried egg, and a piece of ham. They gobble the first biscuits with gulps of milk before leaving with a rag wrapped jug of water in one hand and their second biscuits in the other.

Rita's heart is full of pride as she watches her boys head down the road toward the Smith farm. They remind her of her pa—he was a hardworking man and an early riser. Luke is the type to put work off until tomorrow, or never.

She shakes her head and mutters. "I was such a child when Luke came along. He took advantage of my ignorance, but I'm not sorry—I have two wonderful boys."

Doctor Tom steps into the kitchen. "Rita, did you say something to me?"

She laughs. "I was talking to myself, thinking how proud I am of my boys. They are the only good that came from spending time with Luke. I don't wish anything bad for him, but to be honest, I'm glad he didn't come back. As soon as I can afford it, I want to talk to a lawyer and get a divorce. Do you think getting a divorce will be a problem?"

"It should be no more than a matter of filling out paperwork and presenting it to a judge, but I'm not a lawyer. Your lawyer may have to put a notice in the paper and require a waiting period allowing Luke to show up and protest or agree. Although the church elders will ask if you have a biblical reason for a divorce."

"Yes, I do. I've heard tell of several women he's been with, and he bragged to me of one."

She pours coffee and sits across from the doctor while he eats. "Betty's still asleep. She was restless last night and mumbled in her sleep, but she got up one time. I dread the time when her babies are born. She's getting so large. I was hoping they would be small and easier to deliver. She's too young to be having a baby."

"I'm worried too. I'm glad you take Betty in the yard to play. She needs exercise, lots of it to build muscle. Her body has too much fat. Her daddy must have kept her locked in that little cabin while he worked. The bigger she gets with those babies, the less she'll want to move."

"I tried to cut down on her cookies, but that's about all that will calm her when she has a tantrum. If I can, I'll start taking her for short walks. She loves to be outside, but hates mocking birds."

He grins and stands. "You wouldn't expect a small bird to go after such a big girl."

"She tore down its nest and squeezed a baby bird to death."

His eyebrows go up. "No wonder it scratched her." He pushes his chair up to the table and steps toward the door. "I need to straighten my office. Patients will be arriving soon."

Someone knocks on the front door as Rita clears the table. She sets a plate in the sink and goes to unlock the door. "Sheriff, is something wrong?"

"I need to talk to Doctor Tom."

The doctor opens the door of his office. "Sheriff, you are out early. Is someone injured?"

The sheriff pushes past the doctor to sits in a big armchair. "I told the mayor and board members that you're planning to leave, and I told them the reasons why. Last night, they were talking to people in town, asking for donations from everyone they thought were able to help. They collected over a hundred dollars for you and got most people to promise to pay all future doctor bills with cash. Also, they got three women to promise to take Betty into their homes for one day a week, and two women volunteered to pay their housekeepers to come over here one night a week to watch her at night. That only leaves the weekend and three nights during the week for you to worry with her."

The doctor laughs loud and hearty. "Haven't the tables turned? How do I know they'll keep their promises?"

"Oh, I think they will."

The doctor leans forward in his office chair. "Before I

consider your proposal, someone has to agree to take Betty on Saturday and be available on Sunday in case I have to deliver a baby or treat someone in their home, and one more person has to watch Betty at night. During the workweek, I don't want to spend two nights in a row with her. In other words, I want someone here on Monday, Wednesday, and Friday nights, and I want a contract drawn up and signed by the board agreeing to those terms."

The sheriff shakes his head. "Well, I don't know."

The doctor looks straight into the sheriff's eyes. "I do know. If they don't agree, I'm moving to Conway, and this town will have Betty twenty-four hours a day, seven days a week. She is not my child, and I have no legal obligation to take care of her."

"I'll tell that to the mayor and the board."

"Tell them if they don't agree to my terms, I'll be in Conway next month. A realtor's already located me a house."

"What about Rita?" He nods his head toward the open door where she stands.

"What about her? If the town's thinking of hiring her to take care of Betty, they can forget it. She has the promise of a job in Conway."

He tosses a book onto his desk and turns with a frown. "Sheriff, this town took me for a fool, and they laughed at me as I struggled to take care of an orphaned girl, and to be the doctor for this town and a great deal of the county. I'm soft-hearted for the oppressed, widows, and orphans, but I'm not a fool. I don't like it when people laugh at my troubles." He shoves his chair back and stands.

"Although your main office is in Conway, you live and spend almost as much time in your home office as you do in the rest of the county. You know what I'm up against, and you know what will happen when this area loses its doctor. People could die before they get to Conway in farm wagons."

Turning away, Rita goes to the kitchen, but worry plagues her all morning. *George and Ben will not like moving to town and leaving our farm and the creek.*

A constant stream of patients travels through the office. The doctor has to excuse himself to get a cup of coffee and to eat a quick lunch. Every person takes longer than necessary, each one wanting information about the doctor's leaving.

Rita recruits a woman from the waiting room to watch Betty while she assists the doctor in setting a broken arm and in sewing up a child's hand that went through a glass window. However, she manages time to cook a good supper for the doctor, Betty, and her boys. She even fills the washtub half full of water and leaves it sitting in the sun for more moonlit baths.

While Rita helps Betty get ready for bed, Doctor Tom rinses the supper plates before sitting to smoke his pipe.

"Rita, I didn't know this job would be so difficult when I hired you, but I've never met a woman who could handle it better. The patients like you and most of them refer to you as a nurse. If we move to Conway, I want to introduce you as my nurse."

"Thank you. I appreciate the compliment. I would like to be a nurse, but I could never afford the training."

"I'll buy you a nursing handbook, and you can get hands-on training while working with me."

"I'll have to rent a house in town for myself and the boys, but I don't want to sell Pa's farm. If I can pay the taxes on it, I'd like to keep it for George and Ben."

"We'll work out a way to pay the taxes, even if I have to borrow the money."

"Oh, I wouldn't want you to do that."

"The wages I owe you are almost enough to pay your taxes."

"I guess I should wait a while longer before seeing a lawyer about a divorce. My expenses will be a lot more in the city."

"I don't want you to wait too long. When I can afford it, I'll speak to one." Rita, with the doctor peering over her shoulder, looks into the room where Betty sleeps curled into a ball with the rag doll.

The boys laugh as they step onto the back porch. Hearing laughter and the heavy boots on the porch, Rita excuses herself to help with the bathwater and fix plates of food for her boys.

The doctor proceeds to his room.

After his bath, Ben sits at the table, almost too tired to eat. "Mama, Mr. Smith told me to drive the team with the wagon, because George is taller than me, and it's easier for him to toss the hay onto the wagon. I had an easy job. Although it was hard staying awake in the hot sun. This afternoon, I asked Mr. Smith if I could toss the hay on the wagon until it got about half full, and then I would swap with George. He said, 'Why, son? You've got the easiest job.' But I told him it wasn't quite fair for me to sit all day while George worked so hard tossing up the hay. He nodded his head and told me to do whatever seemed logical. So I swapped jobs with George on each load before the wagon got half full."

She nods and smiles. "Son, I'm proud of you. I'm sure my pa would have done the same. Pa always did his fair share or more."

George comes inside with a wide grin. "Mama, did Ben tell you that Mr. Smith gave us each a dollar and told us we deserved a man's wages because we each did a man's work?"

"No. He didn't tell me. I'm so pleased with you and Ben. You remind me of Pa. He was a hard-working man."

"This afternoon, Ben threw hay on the wagon until it got about half full, and then I tossed while he drove the team. The last hour was tough because Mr. Smith came to help. He pitched hay on one side of the wagon while I worked on the other. He's tall and fast, but I kept up with my side."

Smiling, Rita pats his shoulder. "Son, eat your supper."

"He's cutting our farm tomorrow but said we could haul on Saturday if the hay dries enough. He grinned and said if the ox is in the ditch, we may need to work Sunday afternoon if you let us. "What do you think he meant? I've never noticed an ox on his farm."

"Son, according to the Bible we're not supposed to work, or work our animals on the Sabbath—that's on Sunday for Christians— but if an ox, or any animal, should fall in a ditch or have an accident we are allowed to pull it out and save it. Likewise, if we have essential work and it can't wait past Sunday, God will forgive us for doing it. God knows you must get the hay in the barn before a rain."

"I understand. If Mr. Smith's hay doesn't dry because the sky is cloudy, then we can haul it on Sunday, so it doesn't lay out, get rained on, and ruined."

"Yes. That's what Mr. Smith was trying to say."

"Will you let us work on Sunday if he needs us?"

"I don't like to, but I will. It's no different than me washing our clothes last Sunday afternoon."

"And God won't be mad at us?"

"I don't think so. Sometimes we need to do things we don't want to do."

7 ~ A Thief

Friday morning, Doctor Tom is in the kitchen for his coffee before it has finished perking. "That coffee smells good. I can hardly wait for a cup."

Rita smiles and takes two cups and two saucers from the cupboard. "It'll be a couple of minutes more. George and Ben ate and left in a hurry. Mr. Smith told them he would pay them to shovel the manure from his barn and chicken house and spread it on his garden. They wanted to earn money for school clothes, but last night they were talking of trying to buy a couple of calves to raise. Of course, they won't be able to keep animals if we move to Conway."

"Did you talk to them about the possibility of moving?"

She lowers her head and wipes at a stain on the cabinet. "I'm sorry; they were so tired, and I thought maybe we wouldn't need to go if the town cooperates with their proposal."

He nods and smiles. "Maybe we won't."

Rita pours coffee, sets sausage, eggs, and biscuits on the table. "I think I would like Conway, but I believe my boys are happier away from a larger town."

"Anyone, listening to those boys talk for a few minutes, can tell they love your farm. The sheriff went out there yesterday. I expect he'll stop by this morning to tell us what he found."

A loud knock rattles the front door.

"I bet that's him now. Did you make enough coffee to share?"

"Yes. I thought the sheriff might come by this morning." She reaches for another cup and saucer.

Doctor Tom hurries to open the door. "Good morning, Sheriff. Come in and have coffee with us."

"Thanks. It smells good." He wastes no time in getting to the table. "I went to Rita's farm yesterday afternoon. A hobo lay asleep in the barn loft. Chicken feathers were scattered over the lot, and he'd cooked a chicken over a fire near the barn. I made him pour water over those coals before I put him on his way north. Two chickens were in the barnyard, but the pens' gate was open. I checked the nests after he left. No eggs were inside."

"We're supposed to have a rooster, eight laying hens, and one setting hen with ten chicks."

The sheriff shakes his head. "I bet he had eggs and fried chicken every day this week. I told him if I caught him in this county again, I'd take him to jail and charge him with theft."

Doctor Tom turns to Rita, "Someone from the town is supposed to be here tonight to stay with Betty. If you prepare a picnic supper, I'll take you to your place, and we'll see if anything else is missing. You and the boys can return here for the night if you're afraid a tramp might still be hanging around."

"What time will someone be here to stay with Betty?"

The doctor's eyebrows wrinkle into a frown. "Sheriff, if that woman's not here by five, we'll drop Betty off at your home."

The sheriff shakes his head with a worried look. "I'm sure she'll be here."

Turning her face away from the sheriff, Rita puts a hand over her mouth to suppress laughter. "I'll have our supper in a basket before five."

Rita removes bedsheets, washes, and hangs them on the line while Betty plays in the backyard with a toy broom marching around and around the clothesline watching for squirrels and birds. A brisk wind dries the sheets faster than Rita can get a clean set ready to hang.

Before noon, all the sheets are dry and on the beds, except for Doctor Tom's—they are folded. On her first day of work, he told her no one is allowed in his bedroom. He removed his sheets, and he will replace them.

For the noon meal, Rita mixes a pan of cornbread, an apple cake, and warms up leftovers from yesterday's supper. She has set the last bowl on the table when the doctor comes in ready to eat.

Betty is exhausted from running around the clotheslines, but she beams with pleasure when Rita tells the doctor how nice it was to have Betty helping to keep the birds from landing on the clean sheets.

While Betty takes an afternoon nap, Rita fries a chicken, makes sweet green beans, and potato salad. She packs it in a picnic basket with the remaining apple cake and a jar of strong, sweet tea.

Rita is eager to get home and see if a stranger got inside the house to steal her pa's gun and the few items passed down to her by her mama and grandparents. She hopes that she has more than one hen and a rooster left. Eggs are essential for feeding growing boys.

At five, Miss Pence knocks on the door. She is a tall thin woman with bobbed hair and seems to have a permanent frown, but her frown melts when Betty takes her hand and smiles. "My name's Betty Ann. I like cookies, but I don't like mean birds. Birds bite. See." She points to a tiny scab on her hand.

Rita shows Miss Pence to the room where her bed and Betty's cot stands. "Betty had her supper, but cookies are in the cupboard, and milk is in the refrigerator."

Doctor Tom tells her, "My office, lab, the three examining rooms, and my bedroom are locked, but make yourself and Betty comfortable in the rest of the house. I should be home by nine, although I could be later if there's a problem at Rita's farm. I have a key, so keep the outside doors locked after dark."

Rita and the doctor climb in the buggy, he clicks his tongue, taps the lines on the back of the horse, and pulls onto the road. The sky is clear, except for a few puffy clouds. "We've had a breeze all day from the southwest. I figure we'll get a shower about Sunday."

"I hope Mr. Smith and my boys get the hay into his barn before we get rain."

"Your boys must be good workers. I've heard Calvin Smith is a hard taskmaster."

"George and Ben like him. They are awful tired when they come home, but he seems fair in paying them for their work. They appreciate the chance to earn money—where else could eleven and twelve-year-old boys get jobs."

"I doubt they could find any around here. Grown men tell me there are no jobs to be found."

The doors and windows of Rita's house are still secured, but they can see handprints on every windowsill. "Rita, you're lucky he didn't break a window to get inside."

"I feel fortunate, and I'm glad my garden is not dead. I need to water it before I do anything else. I see a few blooms on the peas."

With a gasp, she leans forward, staring at the onion row and glances up at the apple tree. "Someone has pulled all my big onions, and picked the fall apples." She kicks at a clod of dirt. "I planned to make apple butter with those apples, and some of the onions had seed heads. I always save the seed. This type of onion is so sweet you can almost eat them like an apple. Mama's family has saved the seed for many years."

The doctor points. "There, beside the garden, are the stems and seed heads. We can gather them and let them dry in the barn."

"I hope the onions were not pulled too early to make good seed."

"I'm sorry you had to be gone to take care of Betty. If the town people follow through with their promise to pay me, I'll buy you a bushel of apples and onions too, but I doubt we can find sweet onions or the seed for ones like you had."

Shaking her head, she says, "It's not your fault. Hungry people have to eat what they find. I'm glad he ate the apples instead of breaking into my house."

"I think more than one person was here. Maybe even a family. Look at those small footprints in the garden. I'm going to walk to the creek and see if I can find where someone's camping."

"Oh my. Do you think hungry children are living in those woods?"

"Could be."

While Doctor Tom is gone, Rita draws water to fill both of her washtubs. The boys may want to bathe in the creek, but if they do, she can use the water for doing laundry in the morning.

She draws bucket after bucket of water for soaking the ground around her garden plants and digs grass from another row so she can plant turnips. Smiling, she remembers her mama saying, "Late August, before the first big rain of fall, is the time to plant turnips for winter eating." She scatters the seed and rakes a thin layer of soil over the tiny black specks to prevent birds from feeding on them.

Going into the chicken pen, she calls to her hens and scatters a handful of corn. The rooster and three hens, flapping their wings, descend from a hickory tree and land at her feet. Rita continues to call, and at last, a mother hen runs from the brush near the barn—ten small chicks follow. Rita tosses a few more grains of corn on the ground before closing the woven wire gate.

Rita stands talking to her, hens, "Maybe you can produce enough breakfast eggs to feed my boys, and perhaps some of these chicks will be grown and laying eggs before next spring."

Looking toward the creek, she sees Doctor Tom walking up the hill, taking long strides. With all her troubles, she has never stopped to notice what a handsome man he is—tall and slender with dark hair and blue eyes—but his gentle ways are more attractive to Rita than outward appearance. *He will make some woman a good husband.*

"Rita, signs show that a family's been living near the creek, there's a lot of footprints, but I think the people are gone now. At least one child was with them." He grins and runs a hand through his hair. "They ate your apples and didn't waste a bit. I found cores eaten down to the seed and stem."

"It makes me sad to think of children living in the woods without a home. I don't feel bad about the missing apples. If I had been home, I would have helped gather them for the children."

Doctor Tom stands straight with hands in his back pockets. "You have a beautiful place here. The rolling hills are clear except near the creek, where tree roots help to prevent erosion. Did your pa farm all this?"

"Yes. What Pa didn't have in crops—corn, oats, and wheat— he fenced for pasture. After Pa got sick, Luke didn't do much, and my boys weren't big enough for farming. I hope I can save this land for George and Ben. Now, they're taking an interest in working it."

"Mr. Smith hasn't mowed the fields near the creek. There's some good hay down there; most of it's still green. I'm sure he'll want to mow it later."

"Pa always got two cuttings from the low meadow. I started helping haul hay when I was about the same age as my boys."

"This is an excellent farm, with several acres of rich bottomland."

"Yes. Before the depression, I had several offers from men wanting to buy it. Luke wanted to sell it and move to Kansas City, but I refused. We had a terrible fight over this land— several fights. He threatened to sell it without my consent. But, Pa had the deed changed to my name before he died, and Luke couldn't do a thing with it."

She pauses and looks toward the road as if watching for George and Ben. "At one time, I got afraid Luke might try to kill me and take the farm, but the boys were still little and needed someone with them every hour. Luke didn't like responsibility."

"I didn't see any farm equipment. Did you sell it after your pa died?"

She shakes her head. "It disappeared. I never knew Luke was selling it until it was gone. Pa left me with a good herd of cattle, as well as two horses and two mules. I knew how to run the farm and take care of the animals, but like the farm equipment, Luke sold off the animals or lost them to gambling debts. With what Pa taught me and left me in material goods, my boys and I could have survived off this farm, but Luke stripped it clean before he left. I didn't expect him to come back. He will cause problems if he ever does show up, that's why I want to get a divorce decree as soon as possible."

"I understand. All the time you've worked for me, I thought you were grieving for your husband."

She shakes her head. "I've tried not to say anything negative about Luke, in front of the boys, but I find it hard to say anything good of him."

Looking across the farm with a sigh, a film of sadness covers her face. "I try to use Pa as a good example for George and Ben. Pa was a good man. The only bad feeling I hold against Pa is his forcing me to marry Luke. Pa didn't know the whole story of Luke and me, and I didn't know how to tell him. At fourteen, I didn't understand the meaning of rape—such words were not in my vocabulary."

"You were still a child."

"I was ignorant of science. I didn't even know I was pregnant until Pa got the preacher's wife to explain things to me."

Hugging herself, Rita turns to look toward the mountain. "While she tried to explain how I had sinned and that to make things right for me and my baby's sake, I had to marry Luke. I sat staring into space, wanting to scream that Luke forced me, but the words never came out of my mouth. Before things became clear to me, I was married."

"How old were you when your mama died?"

"Eleven. We lived outside of town, on this farm, and I didn't have friends to visit. Pa was sad after Mama died, and stayed away from the house most of the time, working on something. Before she got sick, Mama taught me to cook and keep the house clean. I milked the cow, fed the chickens, took care of the garden, and helped Pa with the hay. I went to school during the winter months and came straight home to do my chores. I had an isolated life, and Luke kept showing up when Pa was away."

She laughs, a hollow laugh. "I knew the animals had babies, but I just thought God let them know when it was time. Do you think there are many girls as dumb as I was?"

"You weren't dumb, just uninformed. Quite a few girls, from good Christian families, learn the hard way. When parents don't explain the facts of life, many girls find out as you did. Someday, I hope schools will teach those things with a Christian perspective. Often, young girls don't know when to step away."

"We learn from the Bible that we are not supposed to hate, but if I didn't have my sweet boys, it would be hard not to hate Luke. I pray that Luke will someday give up his sinful ways and become a Christian, but maybe my prayers are not strong enough with faith that Luke could change."

8 ~ A Happy Place ~

Rita dusts her hands, picks up a bar of soap, and dips into a pan of water beside the well. "I'll wash up and put our supper on the outside table. I have no idea what time the boys will get here, but we can eat without them."

Doctor Tom asks, "Don't you think we should open the windows to let in some air? If we don't, it'll be awful stuffy in there tonight for you and the boys."

"That's a good idea. I've been watering and didn't think of opening windows." She reaches to push away a strand of hair from the braid wound around her head. "Give me a minute to pin this out of my eyes. I was slapping at chickens flying over my head and knocked some pins from my hair."

"Why not let it hang loose, down your back? It's a pretty color. My mama's hair was brown with shades of red like yours."

Rita feels her face flushing. "I'll only be a minute." Walking into her bedroom, she removes the remaining pins, runs a brush through the long strands, and fastens a clasp on each side of her head above her ears — perspiration beads on her forehead before she can step into the kitchen.

The doctor stands in the doorway with a smile. "Your hair is even more beautiful than I imagined."

The heat in her face seems to expand through her body. Grabbing a cardboard fan from a shelf, she flutters it fast. "Thank you. This heat is stifling. Let's go outside for a few minutes before opening more windows."

He follows her to the yard. "I didn't mean to embarrass you, but I've often wondered how your hair would look hanging down your back."

The fan she holds flutters faster. "I . . . I'm not used to compliments. I don't know how to respond."

"Until today, I always thought you were waiting for your husband to return, so I never allowed myself to show anything other than formal respect for an employee."

"But . . . I'm still married."

"I'm well aware of that. I want to go into Conway on Monday and talk to a lawyer. After you get the divorce, will you allow me the privilege of courting?"

Her mouth drops open, and she gulps a breath of air. "I've never thought of such an opportunity. My first thoughts were of taking care of my boys." She stops fanning to stare at his face. "Yes. Courting will be nice after I get a divorce decree. Until then, I'm only an employee. I don't want anyone accusing us of adultery."

"Neither do I." He smiles and leans against a well post. "Rita, you are a beautiful woman, a wonderful mother to your boys, and more than kind to Betty. I don't understand why you haven't had men standing in line at your door."

"I'm a married woman. I've tried to step away from single men. Since my boys were born, I've wanted the best for them. Luke was not a kind, thoughtful husband or dad. I wanted to avoid anyone who might be like him. I knocked on your door because I needed a job. At first, I didn't know you were single. I asked the grocer about a job, and he told me you wanted to hire someone to greet patients and help with housework. I expected the new doctor in town to be married."

He grins, and his blue eyes seem to flicker. "Before you came inquiring regarding a job, a young woman came by dressed as if she was going to a party. A patient came in while she sat in my office, but she continued to sit giggling and to tell me of her many boyfriends. I got up, stood at the door, and stated, 'Thank you for stopping by. I have a patient to attend. I'll call at the address you gave me if I need more information.' She left with a frown. You came in an hour later, and I knew right away that you were the type of woman I wanted to hire."

She smiles with a faint blush. "How did you know?"

"You asked about the job instead of telling me about your social history. You didn't frown or shake your head at any chore I mentioned, even when I said it would be your job to clean up after sick or bleeding patients. You agreed to work all the hours necessary. You admitted to being a good cook, as long as I didn't expect fancy gourmet dishes. Also, you told me you had two boys, eleven and twelve years old, and if one got sick, you might need to bring them with you and put the sick one to bed, or on a pallet."

Looking down at her hands, she breathes deep. "I was afraid to tell you that, afraid you might tell me I'd have to get someone to watch a sick child at home."

"I felt you were honest."

She clears her throat and looks into his eyes. "Doctor Tom, I think you are a handsome man, a very nice man, but I don't want a courting relationship to interfere with my job. I need this job to provide for my boys. They come before anything else."

"I count that a credit. Children should come first to a mother. My mother put the welfare of her children first, but I could tell she loved my pa just as much. God gave humans a heart and a mind with an unlimited capacity for love."

Sitting on the bench near the door, Rita continues to fan herself, not knowing how to respond to his last comments.

"Stay there and cool down. I'll go open the rest of your windows before we have our picnic."

When he returns with the picnic basket, he brings two plates, two forks, and two glasses for the tea. "I'm hungry, but after we eat, maybe you'd like to walk to the creek. Earlier, I noticed fish swimming in the biggest pool."

"That would be nice, or you might want to walk up to what I call the peak. From the crest, you can see for miles. It has a beautiful view. If I had a talent for painting, I would paint the view looking west near sunset. The red sky hanging around the blue mountain with the meadow and creek in the valley should make a beautiful painting."

He smiles and hands her a plate. "I want to see it. I used to paint, but my paint has most likely dried up. I haven't opened the box since I enrolled in medical school."

They eat and set the basket inside before starting up the path toward the peak.

Near the hilltop, they stop and look toward the creek. "I'm glad you told me about this place. We're not to the crest, but this view is fantastic."

"We'll have to bring a picnic sometime. I like this place better than the creek. As a child, I spent hours under that big oak. At first, squirrels dropped acorn hulls on me, but after a while, they accepted my presence and scampered all around."

They continue to the top and turn to look across the valley. "This is my happy place. After my mama died, I came here almost every day. I felt closer to heaven on this hill, but I've never brought anyone else up here."

"Not even Luke?"

She shakes her head. "No. Luke would have degraded it."

He reaches to take her hand. "I'm honored. Does that mean you think I'm special?" He grins and tilts his head to the side.

She nods, with a somber look. "I know you are special. Still, a courting relationship frightens me."

Rubbing the top of her hand, he looks into her eyes. "Why do I frighten you?"

Shaking her head, she shrugs. "I don't know. Maybe after my experience with Luke, I'm afraid to trust a man, even you."

"But you brought me to your special place. And it's a charming location. I don't remember seeing any site more beautiful."

Rita withdraws her hand, sits on the edge of a large flat rock inside the oak tree's shade, and looks up at him with a smile. "Maybe it can always be our happy place."

"I hope so. When your divorce is final, I want to come here with you, but until then, when we're around other people, we'll act like we don't even like each other."

Rita laughs. "We'll have to work at it. I'm not good at hiding my emotions. Mama used to tell me that she could read my face like a book."

"We may be so tired trying to deal with Betty that we won't have to pretend." He sits on the rock beside Rita.

"She can be a trial at times, but the last couple of days she's been better. I'm wondering what we'll do when her babies are born?"

He shakes his head, "Betty doesn't know she's going to have a baby, and you are the only person who knows I can hear two heartbeats. One is weak and, although she's getting large, I think the babies are smaller than they should be. Before she came to us, I doubt her Pa made sure she ate right. I have my doubts that she'll go full term."

"Are you saying the babies may not survive?"

"They may not. Small babies have a poorer chance of survival. I hope she goes full term. It is all in God's hands."

"At times, she's so sweet that I want to pull her onto my lap and rock her. However, I know when she has a temper tantrum, she could kill an infant within seconds, as she killed that baby bird."

He takes a deep breath. "We'll deal with it the best we can. God may take care of it for us, or he may think we need more lessons in patience. I'm not trying to plan it. I only ask for God's mercy and guidance."

She nods. "That's all we can do." Lifting her hand, she points toward the west. "Look at the sunset. It's almost blood red and reflecting on the creek. See what I mean about beautiful."

"Indeed, I do. Thank you for bringing me up here, and for trusting me to share your special site."

He reaches for her hand. "Now, it's our happy place."

She glances up at the sky. "I think we should be going. It'll be dark soon, and the boys may be home and wondering where I've gone."

When they reach the flat ground near the house, he releases her hand. "I'll be late getting in the office on Monday, but you can open the doors as usual. I don't have an appointment until one, so if I leave at daylight and trot the horse both ways, I should be home from Conway on time. Do what you can to handle any emergency, and tell the drop-in patients to come back in the afternoon."

"If you have to make a house call tomorrow, bring Betty out here. I'll be glad to watch her."

"Thanks, but Saturday is my day to read and catch up on any new medical procedures. I hope Betty will play with her toys, eat cookies, and nap in the afternoon."

Rita chuckles. "I think you are dreaming. She'll eat her share of those cookies I baked yesterday, and she may nap in the afternoon if you keep her busy all morning, but don't count on it too much."

He grins. "I may take Betty for a long walk in the morning."

Do you want me to come over and get her ready for church on Sunday?"

"No. I think we can manage."

"I'll try to save you both a seat close to the church's side door, in case you are running late."

Tom answers with a nod and a wink.

9 ~ The Town Pays

Monday morning, Rita arrives at work before the sun rises, but the sky is fading. Doctor Tom, his buggy hitched to go, grins as she walks toward him on the flagstone walk. "I hoped you would be early. I'm ready to get our plans in motion. Betty's waiting on the porch." Winking, he taps the lines to Dolly's back.

George and Ben follow about two hundred feet behind Rita—dressed in overalls to work in the yard and garden. Doctor Tom promised to pay each of them to pull weeds in front of his office, and to replant chrysanthemums spreading beyond the flower beds behind his house. He also wants Romaine lettuce and turnips planted in his garden.

Rita fries eggs and biscuit dough, and sets out a jar of plum jam someone left the doctor instead of his fee for doctor services.

Ben fills a biscuit with jam and takes a bite. "Mama, these fried biscuits are good. If they're not hard to make, fry them often."

Nodding, Rita smiles and fills a biscuit with jam for Betty.

The girl wiggles in her chair. "Betty like biscuits."

"You boys need to hurry. Eat your breakfast, and get to work."

Betty crams the rest of her biscuit in her mouth and gulps her milk. "Betty work too." She slides from her chair, grabbing George's arm on the way down, smearing jam from his elbow to his hand.

"Betty, your hand is sticky. You got it on my arm."

"Sorry, George. Sor-ry."

Rita washes his arm and Betty's hands with a dishcloth and tosses the cloth into a pan of warm soapy water.

Ben grins at his brother and keeps several feet away from Betty.

George whispers to Rita, "Mama, how can we work with her in the yard?"

"Give her the little broom, ask her to walk back and forth across the yard guarding you and Ben, and keeping the mockingbird away from you. Brag on her every few minutes and tell her she is helping."

The sheriff stops by and asks, "Where has the doctor gone so early this morning?"

"He told me he has some business to attend. I didn't question him. He has several appointments this afternoon. I'm sure he'll be here on time. Can I help you with something?"

"Maybe a cup of your good coffee. I just wanted to see how Betty got along with Miss Pence."

Reaching for the coffee pot, Rita answers, "I didn't ask him. He was in a rush to leave for Conway."

The sheriff's eyes open wide. "Conway? Conway? Is he still thinking about taking a job in Con-way?"

"I didn't have a chance to talk to him this morning. He was ready to leave when I got here."

The sheriff's cup rattles against the saucer as he picks it up to take a sip of coffee. "Had those tramps taken anything else from your farm?"

"They stripped all the fruit from the apple tree and pulled a lot of my onions. The footprints in the garden and around my apple tree looked like they were made by a kid. So don't worry. I don't begrudge food for a child."

Rita refills his coffee cup. "Sheriff, I know Doctor Tom needs cash to pay his expenses. Conway is willing to pay to get him down there. If this town doesn't pay up, and soon, he'll be gone. My boys like it here, but I have to go where I have a job to pay my bills."

The sheriff empties his cup. "Tell the doctor, I'll see him in the morning. Maybe, with all the money. Thanks for the coffee."

"Wait a minute, Sheriff. When are the women going to start watching Betty? You told us three women promised to take Betty to their homes for one day a week."

"I don't know. I'll find out."

From a window, Rita watches him rush down the street toward the mayor's office. She turns to a batch of yeast bread she was mixing before he came in. Setting the dough aside to rise, she rubs a brisket with brown sugar mustard and puts it in the oven to bake.

The doctor arrives at the office a few minutes before one. His appointment is ahead of schedule. He winks at Rita, and says, "The prospect looks good with only a short wait. Make me a sandwich if you will. I'll sneak a few bites between patients."

That morning, Rita soaked a woman's sprained arm in Epsom salt, tied a sling around the woman's arm, suspending it from her neck to keep her arm immobile. Before she left, Rita gave her instructions to soak it every four hours and put the sling back on after every soak.

Rita also doctored bee stings with baking soda patches and gave a woman two aspirins for a headache. She didn't receive any money for her services, but the man with the bee stings left a pint of fresh honey on the doctor's desk.

Rita bakes cookies while Betty takes a nap, and rushes to fix supper so Betty won't stuff herself with cookies and spoil her meal.

At five, the doctor locks his front door and heads for the kitchen. "That brisket on the yeast roll was delicious. Could you make me another one for supper while I tell you about my trip to Conway?"

"Yes, I'll do that. Did you receive good news?" Rita slices a roll and reaches for the brisket.

"The lawyer was a man my pa treated and healed years ago. After I told him you were my employee and a special friend, he said there would be no charge for getting your divorce decree, but you'll have to go to Conway and stand before a judge to get the declaration. He'll let me know when you have to appear. You can drive my horse and buggy to go meet with the judge."

George and Ben come rushing inside. "Doctor Tom, we did all the things you asked us to do."

"I noticed the front flower bed when I came in at noon. It looks good. Did you water?"

"Everything except the seeds. Do you have a sprinkling can?"

"It should be in the barn. Take a look, but if you don't find it, after supper, I'll go help explore."

The boys hurry, going to look for the watering can.

"Rita, the sheriff stopped me on my way here and handed me a wad of money. When you get to work in the morning, I want you to take enough for your taxes and mine, and pay them before we get more late charges tacked on. When the sheriff gave me the money, I promised not to move to Conway, but he still has to get me a written agreement."

Rita sits across the table from Doctor Tom. "I'm happy we don't have to move. My boys like it here, and so do I."

He covers her hand with his but withdraws it before the boys run inside.

Heavy boots pound the porch as George and Ben rush inside. The screen door hinge squeaks and Ben yells, "We found it. We'll water the seeds after supper. We're starving now. Mama, can we eat?"

Rita laughs. "Wash your hands, and don't forget to give thanks before you dig in. I'll slice rolls so you can make sandwiches." She sets baked beans and coleslaw with homemade dressing on the table.

Betty finishes her sandwich and asks for cookies before Rita can sit to eat. "Betty, did you say a thank you prayer for your food?"

Clasping her hands, Betty bows her head, "God, thank you for cookies. Amen."

The doctor sips iced tea and nibbles a cookie as the children eat. "Rita, don't you think Betty is behaving and talking much better since you've been keeping her?"

She nods and pats Betty's back. "Betty's a good girl. She kept the mean bird away while the boys worked on your flower beds."

Nodding her head, Betty smiles. "Betty, good girl."

"Yes, you are."

Betty rubs her face against Rita's arm and slides from her

chair. "I go watch squirrel jump."

"Okay, but don't try to touch it." Rita reaches to tie the sash on Betty's dress before letting her go.

Rita glances at the door and turns toward the doctor. "Did the sheriff say when the women are supposed to start coming to help with Betty?"

"Next week, but I told him for the first month, I'd rather they take her in the mornings and bring her here after lunch so she can take a nap on her cot."

Rita nods. "That should work well."

"I hope it doesn't cause you too much work, but I don't want her getting overtired or agitated. Stress might send her into labor before her time."

"I agree. Now that we are acquainted, we get along fine."

Facing the doctor, Rita asks, "Does she still keep you awake a lot at night?"

"I close my door on the nights you and the boys are here. On weekends, when you go home, I leave my door ajar, and I wake up once or twice each night as she treks into the bathroom. I don't get up, but I leave a light on so she's not frightened. She always goes right back to bed. We may not need someone to stay with her at night. She knows this is her home, and she's not afraid."

Rubbing her fingers across her forehead, Rita looks at the doctor with a frown. "I'm almost afraid to let her go away with strangers. Remember, how anxious she was the first few days after coming here."

He nods. "Maybe the women will come here to watch her for

the first couple of weeks. They can take her for walks and play in the yard until noon and go home while Betty eats with us."

"I think that's a good idea. Betty's first few days with us, I thought she might be more than I could handle, but now I enjoy having her here—most of the time." Rita grins. "She still has her stubborn moments."

"I'll talk to the sheriff relating to women coming here. I'll go over there now. He should be home. Are you and the boys still worried about someone hanging around your farm?"

"No. Not at all. As soon as the boys finish in the garden and I get this kitchen cleaned, we'll be on our way. I think the sheriff took care of the hobo problem. I'll try to be early tomorrow and fix your coffee and breakfast before I go to Conway to pay the taxes."

He smiles and squeezes her hand. "I'll see you in the morning."

Watching him leave, Rita whispers, "Lord, thank you for all my blessings."

The sun hangs low over the mountain when Rita and her boys arrive home. She digs in her purse for a door key. "Boys, I'll open all the windows before I draw water for the garden. Unless you want to take baths in the washtub, get on your way to the creek. I want you back here within thirty minutes, so grab a clean pair of pants and run. It'll be dark soon."

George looks toward the creek and up at the mountain. "I'll take the tub tonight. The bucket in the house is full. That's enough warm water for a bath if there's some in the teakettle."

"Okay, dump the bucket. I'll refill it from the well."

George goes for the water bucket while Ben pulls off his boots. As soon as the water is in the tub, Ben slips out of his overalls and jumps in.

George yells, "You scamp. You waited until I got it ready, and you jumped in." George grabs the bucket of cold water Rita released from the well-bucket and throws it over his brother.

Ben screams and shakes his body. "At least I got to sit in the warmer water for a minute." Laughing, he stands and grabs his towel. "Okay, brother, the tub is all yours."

Rita laughs with the boys. "George, get your boots off. I'll go open the windows while you bathe. When finished, you boys dump the water on the high end of those garden rows so it will drizzle along the middles. Draw more until all the garden gets water."

As she goes about her chore, she hears laughter and splashing. "Boys," she yells, "Have your fun, but don't trample those garden plants. And wash the mud off your feet before you step into my kitchen."

A cool breeze wafts in the living room window as Rita fans her dress tail to dry the water spilled on it. Glancing up, she sees a man walking along the edge of the hay meadow. He has on a floppy hat, and his walk looks familiar. He steps behind a bush and remains standing. After recovering from the surprise of seeing a man on her private land, she runs to the kitchen door. "Boys, grab your clothes and get in the house."

"We haven't finished watering."

"Forget the garden. Get in here. Now!"

10 ~ An Intruder

Detecting fear in Rita's voice, George and Ben grab their dirty clothes and towels. Rushing inside, they ask, "What's wrong, Mama?"

"I saw a man walking along this side of the meadow, and staring at the house. You boys need to sleep in my room again tonight. Help me close all the windows. Later, we may have to open one to get a little cool air. If we do, I'll guard that window with the shotgun."

To prevent anyone from raising the old farmhouse windows, the boys jam shortened broomsticks over the top sections, but they need one more to have enough for the entire house. Instead of a shortened stick for her window, Rita has been using a long-blade butcher knife. With the blade inserted in one of the narrow side gaps, it is difficult to lift the window.

The sun has dropped behind the mountains. The moon is not yet visible, but every bush looks eerie in the darkening twilight. Rita motions for the boys to get on the pallet she spread near her bed. Seeing her hand, they get down without a sound. Rita sits on the edge of her bed, waiting—with a loaded gun to defend her sons.

A tree frog makes loud, irritating shrieks in the big oak tree near the house. Still, Rita hears a twig break under a man's foot. Breathing shallow, she rests the gun on her lap and stares at the closed window. Perspiration trickles along the side of her face as she rubs her hands against her dress and returns them to the gun.

It can't be much later than nine, but people in farming communities rise early and go to bed when the sky turns dark. Detecting the restless breathing of her boys, she knows they are not sleeping even though she woke them that morning at four. *I hope George forced the butcher knife in good and tight. I need to buy a heavy dowel for this room.*

Her hands twitch as a shadow moves in front of the window. A knife glistens, the screen rips against a blade, and a man's hand tugs at the window. The window slides upward, screeching against the butcher knife.

Rita raises the gun and aims as a muscular arm reaches through the opening, followed by a husky shoulder. She pulls the trigger.

A yell follows the blast of her gun, and the man falls backward onto the ground. The tree frog is silent, but the man in the dirt bellows, "Help me! Help me, Luke!"

Someone mutters, "Hush if you want help. That gun has two barrels."

Listening as two men stagger across the yard, Rita whispers to her sons, "Stay down." She reloads the discharged side of her double-barreled shotgun and continues to sit on the side of her bed. "If they try again, I'll empty both barrels, but I doubt they'll be back. I loaded the gun with slugs. The one I shot needs to find a doctor."

"Boys, the window's broken and the screen's cut. I don't have anything in here to cover it, and we don't need to go outside until daylight." She pulls her rocking chair into the bedroom and sits. "Boys, you can sleep on my bed if you want. "I'll sit here with this gun until sunrise."

Ben crawls onto the bed and curls around a pillow. George stands to stare at the window. "Mama, I'll sit up with you if you want."

"No, son. I'll be fine. You get some sleep. I may need you to help watch Betty tomorrow."

"Are you sure?"

"Yes, get some sleep."

George slides onto the bed beside his brother. "Mama, wake me if you get too sleepy. We can talk and stay awake."

"Okay, son, but I think I'll be fine."

The tree frog resumes his horrible song, an owl hoots in the distance, and Rita trembles for a long time. After a while, she yawns, rocks in the squeaky old rocker, and then goes to make a pot of coffee. She drinks half of it before hearing horses approaching, and a knock at the door.

The sheriff's voice calls, "Miss Rita, are you and your boys okay? Mr. Smith said he heard a gunshot over this way."

Opening the door, Rita invites the sheriff and Mr. Smith inside to show them the window and tell them what happened. Her boys move restlessly but remain asleep.

Rita recalls the incident. "I heard the intruder say, 'Help me, Luke.' The other one said, 'Hush if you want help. Her gun has two barrels.'"

She offers coffee and chairs. "I believe one of them was my husband. It may sound strange to you, but I think he came to kill me so he could sell this farm. Luke is lazy, and he has no sympathy for anyone's pain and suffering. If you don't find them soon. Luke may finish killing his friend to keep him from talking, and he'll come back to kill me. I know it sounds cold and ruthless, but that's the way Luke is."

"Where did you shoot him, Miss Rita?"

"I was aiming at his shoulder, but he ducked to come through the window. I might have hit his head."

"There's only a sliver of the moon tonight. It's hard enough to find tracks in daylight and almost impossible on a night like this. We'll get together a posse to start tracking at first light."

"Sheriff, do you think it will be safe for my boys and me to walk into town in the morning?"

Mr. Smith says, "I'm too old to ride this rough country with a posse or drag my bad leg through the woods looking for an outlaw. Tomorrow's my day to pick up feed, so I'll be here at six-thirty in my wagon to take you to town, or I'll drive you in now if you want."

"Thank you, Mr. Smith. My boys are asleep, so I'll wait. On most days, I enjoy the walk into town, but tomorrow riding will be better."

The following morning, in the murky dawn, Ben finishes watering the garden while Rita and George find boards and nail them over the broken window. Mr. Smith arrives as expected at six-thirty, ready to start toward town.

Doctor Tom is shocked at the news. "Rita, no patient with gunshot wounds knocked on my door during the night. Things around here were peaceful, but it disturbs me to hear someone tried to break into your home. I want you to stay here until the sheriff catches those two criminals. After breakfast, I'll take the buggy and go to pay our taxes. I don't want you being a target for a deranged husband or his hitman."

Rita, her boys, and the doctor gather around the kitchen table talking of the night's excitement while coffee perks.

With a gasp, Rita rips off her apron and runs for the door. "I've got to tell the sheriff something before he leaves."

His eyes wide, Doctor Tom points at George. "You boys stay here with Betty until we get back." The door slams behind him, as he runs to catch up to Rita.

Six men on horses wait outside the sheriff's home. Doctor Tom follows Rita inside.

"Sheriff!" Rita gasps, "Along the creek running through my farm, there are two places where an overhanging bank could be dropped to bury someone. They are both on the right side when riding west within the creek. I warn my boys not to walk under those places, and you need to avoid passing underneath. After all this dry weather we've been having, your horses can walk in the creek without being in danger."

He stares at her. "Do you think Luke may have buried his partner alive?"

"Alive or dead. If one of those banks shows the result of a recent cave-in, I think you should investigate. Also, half-way between those two places is a secret cave. It's visible above a big flat rock. During a rainy season, the creek covers the opening, but during dry seasons the big rock holds water in the cave, and the water's deep. A giant catfish lived there when I was a kid. I stopped going in from the creek after I noticed the fish. It was so big it reminded me of the Bible story about Jonah and the whale." She catches her breath before continuing.

"The cave has a second entrance inside a circle of sassafras trees on the hill above it. I noticed Luke going into those trees a couple of times, so I know he is aware of the cave. Those two men could be hiding there."

"Mercy, girl, we need to get on our way."

"Sheriff, if you find those men before you get to the cave, I wish you wouldn't say anything to your men. My boys take great pleasure in having a secret Indian cave."

He nods. "I'll keep their secret if I can."

"I hope you catch them. Maybe you can follow a blood trail from my window."

Walking back to his house, Doctor Tom says, "Rita, you amaze me. You seem so gentle and feminine, yet you shoot a man coming in your window and stay in the house guarding your boys for the rest of the night."

Rita laughs. "It was not peaceful. For an hour, I sat trembling and wishing I had one of those expensive repeater rifles. I was scared, and I still am. I think Luke wants me dead. I need a divorce, so he can't take Pa's farm away from my boys."

"How many acres do you have?"

"A hundred and eighty on the south side of the creek and twenty more on the north that Pa bought before Mama died. I never told Luke Pa owned the twenty. It's a wooded area with a few deer living inside. Luke wanted to kill the deer, and he would have hunted them if he'd known the land didn't belong to someone else. My boys and I love to watch the deer gathering at the creek to drink and grazing in the meadow late in the day."

"With this drought and a depressed economy, farmland is not selling for much. If I had lots of money, I'd buy all the land I could. I think by the time your boys are our age, your land will be worth a fortune."

"I don't know the value, but there is enough for each one of the boys to have a good farm. Mr. Smith has two hundred acres next to mine, and he doesn't have living children. His son died when a runaway horse fell with him. Someday his farm will be for sale. Most people don't care much for Mr. Smith, but my boys like him and his wife."

Rita finds George and Ben on the porch shelling raw peanuts. One of the doctor's patients left the bag yesterday. Doctor Tom told the boys he would talk Rita into making peanut candy if they shell the nuts.

George scolds, "Betty stop eating them, or you'll have a bellyache, and you won't get any candy."

"How many has she eaten?" Rita asks.

"Every nut she's shelled."

Rita sighs and shakes her head. "Come with me, Betty. We need to go into the house and finish making breakfast before you fill your tummy with peanuts and get sick."

It is late afternoon before the sheriff and his posse return to town. Rita is ready to leave for the store to buy a new window when the Sheriff knocks on the door. Doctor Tom invites him inside. "Did you catch them?"

"The one Miss Rita shot was inside the cave. I'm glad she told us about that place. We wouldn't have found it if we hadn't been looking close. Bushes were almost covering the creek entrance. Afterward, we found the hill entrance surrounded by sassafras trees."

He turns toward Rita and takes off his hat. "Bill Clark is slimmer than the rest of us and wore a holster with a six-gun instead of carrying a rifle. Bill eased down through the hole using tree roots for a ladder and found the injured man, who claimed Luke told him your house belonged to him and that no one lived there. He didn't have a gun, but told us Luke has one." The sheriff shakes his head and frowns.

"The injured man is in a lot of pain. The bullet cut a groove in his cheek and buried in his shoulder. A couple of the boys went to get Mr. Smith to bring the injured man to the doctor in his wagon. They took him out of the creek entrance. He was in too much pain to climb those tree roots. The catfish was still in the cave or another one similar. Like you, those men were afraid to get in the water with that big thing. It will weigh close to a hundred pounds. Bill shot it, and they're bringing it to town in the wagon with the injured man. They want to have a fish fry on the square if women will cook other foods to go with it."

Doctor Tom leaves the room to prepare for the wounded man. Rita asks, "Do you have Luke in custody?"

The sheriff shakes his head. "No, but I sent a man to Conway to notify officials and to telephone all the nearby counties with his description and a stated charge of attempted murder. The man we have in custody said Luke made him walk to the cave and then pushed him in the hole. He didn't remember how he got to the bottom. Bill Clark had a heck of a time getting down through those tree roots, and he didn't have a bullet in his shoulder."

"I hope you catch Luke." Rita sighs. "I'll not sleep well until he's behind bars."

The sheriff shakes his head. "I expect he's miles away from here by now. Didn't you say he's from Louisiana and that he still has relatives living down there?"

She nods. "Yes, the last I heard that's where Luke's folks lived."

"Do you remember the name of a town?"

She frowns and shakes her head. "No, I'm sorry. I can't remember the name of the town."

The sheriff nods. "Anyway, I'll make some calls down there."

The Doctor's Luck

11 ~ Attempted Murder

Rita has washed the breakfast dishes and sent the children outside by the time Mr. Smith arrives with the injured man. Standing in the hall watching as men take him to the doctor's examining room, Rita notices his tan shirt is stained with blood. She remembers that the man in her meadow had on a blue shirt.

Mr. Smith steps near her in the hallway. "After picking up the man and the fish, I told the men with the posse to take that fish to my hog-killing shed, get it cut up and soaking in tubs of saltwater before anyone starts to town with it. The salt helps to preserve it, but if they are not going to cook it today, they need to rinse the salt off and put it in a freezer or cooler. The grocer is the only one I know with a cooler big enough to hold so much meat. They'll need someone besides me to ask him." He chuckles. "I'm not on his friend list."

Mr. Smith removes his straw hat and fans himself. "I better get on home. They should have the fish cleaned and cut up by the time I get there. They'll be needing me to haul it to town."

"Will you and Mrs. Smith be going to the fish fry?"

"I reckon so. We love fried fish, and my woman loves a party."

"I'm afraid to be out where Luke can take a shot at me, but my boys will want to go. I don't think he would hurt them, but he might try to kidnap them to get at me."

"Do you want me to keep an eye on them?"

"Yes, if you don't mind. I don't want the boys to miss a good time."

"I'll find out the time and place for it and let you know when we'll pick them up."

"Thank you. I'll bake a cake and prepare a vegetable dish for my boys to take."

Rita decides to wait until another day before going to get a new window. The sky does not look like she needs to worry about rain. She roasts the shelled peanuts, makes chocolate peanut clusters, and has supper warming on the stove when Doctor Tom exits his office.

"That man lost a lot of blood. Sheriff, I hate to move him, but I don't want to be responsible for him. If he stays here, you need to leave a guard to watch him." The doctor takes a peanut cluster from a platter, pops it in his mouth, and lifts two more with a sheet of wax paper and hands them to the sheriff.

"I'll have a couple of men carry him to jail. Then we can all get some sleep."

"Sheriff, I will appreciate it if you can have a deputy watch this house. Rita and her boys are going to stay here tonight. Betty and Rita sleep in the third room from the back of the house—there's a thorny rosebush under their window. The boys have cots in the large storage room, next to Rita and Betty's room; their room doesn't have a window. Mine is the last bedroom at the end of the hall and on the back of the house. I'm a sound sleeper, and Rita's exhausted from being up last night, so if you have any deputies out tonight, please have them keep an eye on this house—especially the bedroom window over that rosebush."

"I'll do that. Everyone, me included, is concerned for Rita and her boys."

After the sheriff leaves, Rita puts Betty to bed. George and Ben help with the dishes and go to their cots to read, but they are soon asleep. The paperback books lay on the floor when Rita looks into their room.

Doctor Tom, pulls every shade in the house and turns out the lamps, except dim lights in the bathroom, hall, and kitchen. "Rita, do you know how to shoot a pistol?"

"Yes." She nods. "Pa taught me, but I haven't seen his pistol since Luke left. I assume Luke took it."

"I keep one in my bedroom, one in my office desk, and one in my medical bag for when I have to go out at night. I'll let you have this one from my medical bag to keep in the lamp table beside your bed."

"Thank you." A tiny smile curves her lips. "I wished that I had brought my shotgun."

He grins and hesitates before continuing. "It's loaded. Make sure you're awake before you pull the trigger. Betty gets up every night to go to the bathroom."

"I will. Pa taught me gun safety."

"If Luke is still running free when we get a notice from the lawyer for you to sign papers, I can't let you drive to Conway alone. I'll have to take a day off and go, or pay someone to drive you."

Her eyes open wide. "Oh. I didn't think of the trip to Conway.

I can't delay signing those papers. I have to go."

"The sheriff has to take the prisoner into Conway for a hearing, as soon as he's well enough to travel, but it might be more dangerous for you to go with them. Luke will want to kill a witness. I'm surprised Luke didn't shoot him before pushing him into that hole. Although, the way that fellow was bleeding, he would have died within a few more hours."

Squinting her eyes into a tired frown, Rita says, "I bet Luke was somewhere watching the cave and knows the sheriff took his partner, or he might have left the state knowing that man would soon bleed to death. I forgot to tell the sheriff that the man I saw beside the meadow had on a blue shirt. I noticed the intruder had on a tan shirt. My observation may not help anything, but," She shrugs. "It might. I'll tell the sheriff tomorrow."

Rita yawns and stands. "I need to get in bed. Things are starting to look blurry."

"Go on to bed. I'll turn out this kitchen light."

Rita starts a prayer but falls asleep, thanking God for blessings.

Near midnight, Betty sits up in bed, mumbling to herself.

Blinking her eyes, Rita focuses on the girl as she stands. At the same time, she hears the click of a gun's safety switch. Rolling from her bed, she lunges at Betty, pushing her onto the bed as a gun roars, and a bullet thuds into the wall. A neighbor's dog barks, and the town seems to explode with loud voices.

Doctor Tom, George, and Ben run to Rita's room as Betty pushes her way toward the bathroom. "Betty go. Betty go."

Knowing that Rita and Betty are okay, Doctor Tom, with a gun in his hand, runs out the front door. Rushing behind him with another, Rita sees the yard is full of men with guns pointing at a stranger—it is not Luke. She returns to check on Betty.

The bathroom door is half-open, and Betty sits on the toilet, crying. "Betty bad. Betty 'fraid, tee-tee on floor."

Rita bends to hug her. "Betty's not bad. Betty's my sweet girl. It's okay to be afraid. A man in the yard made a loud noise. It made me afraid too."

Betty looks up with tearful eyes. "Did Rita tee-tee on floor?"

Rita smiles. "No, but almost."

By the time Rita calms Betty, gets the nervous girl on her cot, and gets George and Ben back in their beds, Doctor Tom returns with the sheriff.

The sheriff drags out a chair, glances at the coffee pot, and takes a note pad from his pocket. "Miss Rita, I need you to tell me what happened."

Rita fills the coffee pot with water, dumps coffee in the percolator basket, and sits. "I was half asleep when I heard Betty stand and heard a gun's safety click. Rolling from my bed, I lunged at Betty, pushing her onto her cot before the bullet hit the wall. I didn't have time to think about hurting Betty. I wanted to get her out of the way of a bullet. The light from the hallway cast her shadow on the window shade. The person in the yard could see her silhouette through the shade, and I'm sure that man thought he was shooting at me."

"He might have, but we've got him in jail now."

"Yes, but Luke is still free to hire someone else to kill me."

The sheriff leans forward to lay a hand on her shoulder. "Miss Rita, people in this town like and respect you. Did you notice how many men were here after a shot rang out? You are one of ours. People want to protect you and your boys. We'll get Luke."

"I hope you get him before he gets me."

It is after one when Rita climbs back in her bed. Betty is asleep, and Rita's boys are quiet. *What must George and Ben think of the things people are saying?* Everyone liked her pa, but it is evident they feel the opposite about Luke.

Before daylight, Rita wakes and goes to the kitchen to make fresh coffee, and knead the dough she left rising the night before. *I'll have to stay busy today, and I'll have to listen and watch for any unusual movements—any stranger could be a killer.*

Wednesday, Mr. Smith cuts the remainder of hay on Rita's farm. Friday, George and Ben go to haul most of it. Saturday morning after the dew dries, they go to move the last of the hay.

Betty is still nervous after the shooting. Doctor Tom tells the sheriff Rita will be staying all week to watch Betty. They will not need women to help until Betty gets over her fear.

Saturday afternoon, Betty is taking a nap when Ben plops onto Doctor Tom's porch near where Rita sits shelling peas. "Mama, Mr. Smith said we'll need hay if we get calves, and we need to get calves growing if we have a herd by the time we graduate high school. He told us to haul the last two loads of hay to our barn."

Rita shakes her head. "Boys, your plans sound good, but I don't have money to buy calves. How will you pay for them?"

George grabs a purple hull pea and shells it into her bowl. "Mr. Smith gave us one. It's just a week old, but its mama fell down a creek bank and broke her leg. He had to shoot her. He's been feeding the calf on a bucket but said he's too old and tired to do that. He gave us the bucket and a sack of powdered milk to mix with water. The calf is already in our barn at the farm. You don't mind—do you, Mama?"

"As a rule, I would be pleased, but now I'm afraid for you to be out of my sight. A baby calf has to be fed every morning and every night, and the sheriff wants us to stay in town where he can keep an eye on us. I didn't worry so much while you were with Mr. Smith, but I don't like you going to our farm by yourselves."

"No one has been shooting at us."

"Oh, boys, I know, but I worry so about you."

Doctor Tom steps onto the porch. "You boys can put your calf in my barn. My mare, Dolly, should love having company. Is it a bull or heifer calf?"

Ben's smile spreads. "She's a little red heifer with a white face."

"Good. Maybe your calf will grow into a cow and raise several calves."

"We're counting on it, but we need another one to keep her company. Mr. Smith promised to ask around and let us know if he finds one for sale."

"Keep in mind that you'll have to buy more milk."

"We know, Mama. We've got twelve dollars saved. We haven't spent a nickel all summer."

Rita frowns. "What about school clothes?"

"We'll be fine with the things Mrs. Smith gave us. We don't care if they are a bit big. We're growing fast."

"Yes, you are. Did Mr. Smith tell you what time he plans to be here to take you to the fish fry?"

"He said six."

She looks up from the peas at two boys dusty and dirty from working in the hayfield. "You need to get baths and rest before time to go."

George jumps up and dusts at his overalls. "We have to go get our calf and feed her before we go. We can't leave her without milk."

"Oh, I don't like for you boys to go out there by yourselves, and we don't have a wagon or trailer. How will you get her here? Our farm is over a mile outside of town."

Ben steps forward. "She's a week old. We can tie a rope on her and make her walk."

"Are you sure she's strong enough for such a walk?"

"She'll have to be."

Doctor Tom says, "I'll haul her in my buggy if you boys will spread gunny sacks on the floor and promise to clean it if she makes a mess."

They grin and nod. "Sure. We'll tie a rope on the calf and hold her so she can't get away."

"All right. Let's go hitch Dolly to the buggy and get some sacks from the crib, but first, I need to get my doctor bag. I don't ever go far without it. I never know when I might need to help someone."

Rita follows the doctor inside. "I'll get the gun for you."

"No. You might need it. I'll take the one from my desk."

"Thank you for helping the boys, and please be careful. I can't help but worry as long as Luke is free."

"I enjoy helping the boys, and I'm always careful." He winks and leaves.

The Doctor's Luck

12 ~ Pain for Mr. Smith

Rita goes inside and locks all the outside doors before putting the peas on to cook. She mixes a cake and slides it in the oven for the boys to take to the fish fry. *I should make another cake—Betty will be unhappy if she sees a cake and doesn't get to eat any.*

She has two cakes, frosted, and peas cooked. One cake and a jar of peas with a serving bowl are packed in boxes before Betty wakes. It is five o'clock, and the fish fry starts at six. Rita can imagine dozens of horrible things happening to her boys and Doctor Tom but tells herself the little calf must have escaped from them. When the clock shows the time is past six, Rita is near panic. Mr. and Mrs. Smith have not arrived to pick up the boys. Again, she reasons that the calf escaped, and they are all trying to find it.

At eight-thirty, the sheriff knocks on the door. "Rita, you missed a good party, but I brought you a box of fish. It's good. He rubs his protruding stomach. I thought your boys were coming with the Smith's."

"Doctor Tom and the boys went to my farm to pick up a calf, and they haven't come back. Will you check on them? I'm about sick with worry."

"Sure. I'll go by my home office and get a deputy to ride along. Don't worry. I bet the calf got away from them."

Rita returns to the kitchen where Betty has finished her supper and dug into one corner of the cake with her spoon. She has chocolate cake on her face, hands, and half of the table. Smiling through the chocolate, she says, "Cake good. Betty like cake."

Praying, Rita cleans the kitchen and Betty. They sit at the table for Rita to read from a book of nursery rhymes. Betty points at pictures and identifies them—"Cat and fid-dle, Cow jump moon, Humpy Dumpy, Bo Sheep."

"Betty, you are smart—smarter than I thought. I've only read this book to you a few times. You need someone to help you learn."

The girl's face glows. "Betty smart."

Betty is asleep in her bed before the sheriff and his deputy ride into the yard.

Her heart racing, Rita peeks from the edge of a curtain and sees her boys riding behind the men. She unlocks the door and flings it open. "What happened to Doctor Tom?"

The sheriff answers. "The doc's fine. Mr. Smith is sick. The doc's with him."

George slides off the horse. "Mama, Mr. Smith is bad sick. We heard Mrs. Smith ringing her dinner bell for help and rode over there. Mr. Smith had gone to feed his cows when his chest started hurting. She saw him sitting on the ground by the gate and went to check on him. He told her to ring the dinner bell, and someone would hear it and come help him get in the house."

Ben steps close. "Mama, Doctor Tom carried Mr. Smith to his bedroom and gave him some white pills. I didn't know Doctor Tom was so strong; Mr. Smith is a big man."

"I hope Mr. Smith will be okay. I worried about all of you."

"Doctor Tom told us to go feed our calf as quick as we could and come straight back to the Smith house before it got dark. He's going to stay with Mr. Smith until tomorrow. We can get the calf another time."

The sheriff ties his horse to a porch rail. "Rita, if you've got a little coffee left in the pot, I could sure use a cup. I'm getting addicted to your coffee."

Despite the worry creasing her brow, with a wave of her hand, she motions for them to come inside. "I believe there's some left. Come on to the kitchen."

The deputy declines the invitation and moves on down the street.

Rita turns on the flame to heat the coffee. "It won't take long to warm." She reaches into the cupboard for a cup, saucer, and three plates. "Boys, the sheriff brought us a box of fish. Do you want to eat some of it now?"

They shake their heads and say, "Just some cake."

The sheriff chuckles. "The same here."

Rita pours milk for the boys and refills the sheriff's coffee cup. "Did Doctor Tom say what he thinks is wrong with Mr. Smith?

The sheriff shakes his head and swallows. "No, but he kept listening to his heart with his stethoscope. My guess is his heart."

"I hope not. The Smiths are kind to my boys. If it's his heart, he'll have to quit working so hard."

Ben sits straighter in his chair. "Mama, he asked George and me to help gather his corn next week. Is it all right with you for us to do that?"

"I guess so, but you've never gathered corn before, and Mr. Smith may not be able to show you how he wants it done. Next week is the last week before school starts. You can't miss school to work."

George lowers his head, but his eyes stare at Rita. "Mama, you used to help Grandpa gather corn. Didn't you?"

"Yes, son, but I have to stay here and watch Betty."

"No, next week, those women are supposed to watch her in the mornings. We don't want you to gather the corn, but if you show us how, we'll do it ourselves. We already know how to hitch up the team, and we took the hay rack off the wagon and put the sideboards on."

"There is not much learning how, but a lot of hard work. You take three rows at a time. Some people take five—two rows on each side, and you run over the middle row with the wagon. The middle row is called the down row because the wagon knocks the corn down, and you have to pick it up off the ground."

Turning her hands over and rubbing them, she says, "You'll need to wear work gloves. Those corn shucks will eat at your hands. Pa always made sure I had good gloves. I doubt that Mr. Smith has gloves small enough to fit you."

"Yes, he does. He bought leather gloves for us to use when we were hauling his hay. The pitchforks were making blisters on our hands."

She grins and nods. "Then all you have to do is wait until the dew dries off and start to work. After a while, you'll develop a way of snapping off the ear with a twist of the wrist. Pa was quick, but my hands and wrists weren't strong. Sometimes I had to twist the ear or break it over my leg. I was a lot slower. Pa gathered two rows and the down row while I harvested one." She pauses to stare at the anxious boys. "I guess I can go for an hour and help you get started."

The sheriff interrupts. "I don't think that's a good idea, Rita. I'll meet your boys in the field at ten-thirty. I've gathered a lot of corn in my life. I can help them. A cake like this one will be enough pay for an hour of work."

Rita laughs. "Is pay in advance fair enough?" She hands him the box prepared for the boys to take to the fish fry. "Don't overeat and get sick before Monday."

He chuckles. "I'll do my best to restrain myself."

Sunday morning, Rita wakes the boys early. "George, Ben, get in here and eat your breakfast. You have to go feed your calf."

Both hurry to the table, gobble their food, and rush for the door. George pauses, "Mama, we'll be back as soon as we can to get ready for church."

"Be careful, boys." Rita watches them run down the walking path. "God, please keep my boys safe, look down on Mr. Smith, and bring back his health. Please watch over Doctor Tom and me, Lord. Keep me safe, so I can raise my boys."

She is trying not to think about what could happen to her boys, Doctor Tom, and Mr. Smith. Rita prepares vegetables for the noon meal and leaves them on the stove, in the pans, so she can warm them when she returns from the church service.

"Betty, come in the bathroom so we can bathe and get ready for church."

When Betty does not answer, Rita goes to her room. Betty sits in the middle of her cot with the ragdoll—it is torn into small pieces. "Bad baby doll. Bad baby tee-tee on bed."

Rita can see a wet circle on the cot. The stained bed doesn't bother her, but the hate and angry look in Betty's eyes sends a chill up her spine. Betty yanks at the doll, pulling apart an arm and spreading cotton stuffing across the bed.

"Betty, we don't hurt babies when they wet things. Babies can't help it. That's why we put diapers on them." Rita gets a dry pair of Betty's underpants from a drawer and smiles at the frowning girl. "Pull off the wet pair of underpants. I've got a nice dry pair for you. When you get the dry ones on, we'll go to the kitchen and have cake and milk. Okay?"

Betty smiles. "I like cake."

"I like cake too. Now, step out of the wet pants."

Betty obeys.

"Sit on the bed and hold up one foot." Rita slips the open leg over Betty's foot. "Hold up the other foot. Good girl. Now stand and pull them up so we can go get cake."

Betty wiggles into the underpants and reaches for Rita's hand. "Go eat cake."

Noticing Betty's red and swollen face, Rita goes to the bathroom for a cold washcloth and washes the girl's face and hands. Betty does not scream and kick as usual but seems to enjoy the touch of the cool cloth. After slicing the cake and pouring a glass of milk,

Rita watches Betty devour her portion of the cake.

"Betty, let's sit in the bedroom rocking chairs, and I'll read you a book."

She nods, but her eyes are squinting.

Gathering the torn doll into a towel, Rita lays it on her bed while she strips the sheets and blankets from Betty's bed and replaces them with clean, dry ones. Before she finishes tucking in the corners, Betty starts to kick and scream, "Read book. Read cow jump moon."

"Okay. Okay, we'll read. Get on your bed. I'll sit beside you and read so you can see the pictures." By the time Rita reads two rhymes, Betty is asleep.

Rita sends George and Ben to the church service without her.

The Doctor's Luck

13 ~ Poison in the Well

Sunday afternoon, Doctor Tom comes home exhausted after staying up all night. "Rita, Mr. Smith's heart was beating normal when I left, but he's always been a hardworking man. The first time he attempts a difficult chore, he may have a heart attack."

"How will he take care of all those cattle? The Smiths have close to a hundred cows."

Doctor Tom grins. "Ninety-eight cows and two bulls. He told me he wants to sell all but ten, three-year-old heifers. I wish he would sell them all."

"He loves his animals, but taking care of them may kill him."

"He wants to pay George and Ben to feed them after school through the winter. Next spring, he'll turn them out to graze. It's a good job for the boys."

"They're going on Monday to gather his corn. I don't like for them to be out in that big field by themselves, but they're growing up, and I have to let go. I pray they'll be safe."

"Luke won't hurt them."

"I hope he has enough morals to keep his children safe."

"How did you make it with Betty at church?"

"I didn't go. I don't know what happened to her, but she was in a terrible mood. I didn't want to take her by myself.

"After I finished cleaning the kitchen, I found her sitting in the middle of her wet cot with that ragdoll she's carried around and loved so much. She was tearing it into small pieces and saying, "Bad baby. Bad baby tee-tee on bed. You should have seen the angry look she gave me when I walked into the room. She looked like some character on the cover of a paperback horror novel, and her face was red and swollen."

He frowns. "It sounds as if Betty's blood pressure might have been high. I need to check it. She may be getting an infection. I hope not. If she can remain healthy for another three or four weeks, the babies should be all right—at least one of them. Where is she now?"

"Taking a nap."

"I need a nap too. I'm going to my room, but as soon as Betty wakes, knock on my door. I want to check her heart and blood pressure."

"I know you are exhausted, but I have to tell you what I witnessed today with Betty makes me feel it will not be safe to have a helpless baby around her. Someone will need to watch her every second after the babies are born."

A sad, defeated look comes over his face. Propping an elbow on the table and leaning his face in his hand, he sighs. "Rita, what are we going to do? When I moved to this town, I expected my luck to get better and better, but it's going downhill. Except for you and your boys."

He shakes his head. "I couldn't make it without you. I would have moved away. I try to be a good man, but I feel like God is punishing me. If He's putting me through trials, I hope He is not expecting too much. I don't think I can tolerate things as Job did."

Rita wants to put her arms around him like she does her boys when they are sad, but instead, she reaches to grasp his hand. "We'll get through this. We have to be strong. God has not abandoned Betty or us. To protect the babies, we may each have to wear a papoose bag with a baby inside."

He looks at her and grins. "Rita, you are a gem." He stands and walks toward his bedroom.

Betty's blood pressure is normal when she wakes from her nap, and she doesn't have a fever. Doctor Tom thinks she may have got frightened, thinking she would be in trouble for wetting her bed. "Her pa may have punished her for wetting the bed."

Things go smooth for the next week. No one in town reports seeing or hearing from Luke and the man Rita shot is transferred to the jail in Conway, along with the one captured outside Doctor Tom's house.

George and Ben gather Mr. Smith's corn and store it in his corn crib. Before and after school, the boys rush to feed their calf that is now in the doctor's barn. The calf is growing and becoming a lovable pet. During the day, it grazes in the lot near Dolly, the doctor's horse, and in the evening, Dolly often nuzzles it through the slats of her stall.

Mr. Smith seems to be doing well and sits on a chair supervising the boys each afternoon as they work around his farm. He wants them to saddle two horses and ride over the farm, count his cattle every day, and get familiar with them. If one is calving, he wants them to know about it and call a neighbor if the cow needs help.

When her boys rush in from school to change into work clothes, Rita has sandwiches ready for them to eat on the way to the Smith farm. She can see her boys are turning into men. Their arms and legs are growing strong with muscle.

Betty is getting large and clumsy, and her temper tantrums are more frequent. She blames someone else when she can't make it to the bathroom in time. If George is in the house, she accuses him of spilling water. He takes it with a grin, telling her he is sorry. Ben always runs out of the house, but George mops up the water.

Most of the women who promised to help with Betty have stopped coming. Some of them are afraid of her, but Miss Pence still comes on Friday nights, so Rita and her boys can go to the farm.

Rita's divorce is pending. She and Doctor Tom wait for a judge to sign the final decree.

On a warm Friday afternoon in October, Rita climbs into Doctor Tom's buggy with a picnic basket in her hand. Betty made it a very trying week. Rita is anxious to leave town and head for her farm. She leans back with a sigh. "I bet my purple hull peas are ready to pick, and the turnips should be big enough to eat."

Doctor Tom smiles. "Rita, this afternoon, a patient left a bushel of peas and a half bushel of turnips in my office. I put them in the cellar. I'll help you shell the peas tomorrow after church."

"Good. I'll take my canner with us tonight and can your peas with the ones I get from my garden—if you can watch Betty. It would be difficult to watch the pressure gauge on a canner and keep up with her demands."

"Don't be too disappointed if you don't get peas from your garden."

"Oh, I'll get some. The vines had hundreds of young peas when we were there last week, and we got a good rain on Wednesday. For a time, I was afraid they might not be ready before frost, but now they should be big and purple."

"Yes, but the chickens were turned out of the pen so they could forage and get water. They may be feasting on your purple hull peas, and the boys said about two dozen geese were in the yard one day before they moved the calf. A bunch of geese can clean a field of peas within a short time."

She frowns. "Oh my. I didn't think about other birds, and the chickens would have died without water and food."

Doctor Tom was right. Chickens are in the garden when Tom and Rita arrive in the buggy. Rita shakes her head with a smile. "At least the chickens look healthy. Maybe we have eggs to gather."

She goes into the hen house with an egg basket she keeps in a large wooden box beside the door. Not one of the nests has an egg inside. Frowning, she looks at the dry ground inside the house. Several large footprints are visible. *Could Luke be living on this farm?*

Lifting the lid to return the egg basket, she notices a clean spot on the floor of the box where she kept a sack of insecticide used for killing bugs in the garden. *Why would anyone steal bug poison?*

Rushing up the path, she sees that Doctor Tom has unlocked the house and is opening the windows. "Doctor, someone has taken all the eggs. I found a man's footprints in the henhouse, and someone has removed a sack of bug poison from a box where I keep the egg basket. Why would someone steal bug poison? Unless?"

Without waiting for an answer, she runs to the well, draws a bucket of water, and releases it into a watering bucket. A powdery substance floats on top of the water. "Someone has poisoned our well."

Doctor Tom steps close to look at the water. "Do you think Luke could do such a thing and maybe kill his children?"

She nods. "Luke doesn't care about the boys. He only cares for himself." Trembling, she takes a deep breath.

"I remember Luke telling me about neighbors feuding with his relatives. He thought it was funny when his Grandpa dumped poison in their well and killed the entire family without firing a shot."

Hugging herself, she says, "I hate for my boys to learn that it's Luke, trying to kill us. Let's close this house, go by the Smiths, and tell the boys to go to your house instead of coming here." She dumps the bucket of poisoned water in the garden before helping to shut the windows.

"Rita, I thought you were too suspicious about Luke wanting to kill you to get your farm, but now I believe it. He is willing to destroy you and his children so he can sell this farm.

On the way to the Smiths' house, Doctor Tom tells her, "Rita, scoot down in the seat and cover yourself with that blanket. If I see someone, you'll need to get down on the floor. We've been coming here every Friday evening. Luke may be watching for us."

Mr. and Mrs. Smith sit in lawn chairs under a large tree. "Come join us in the shade," Mrs. Smith calls.

Doctor Tom pulls close with the buggy. "We'd love to, but we need to get back to town and talk to the sheriff. Someone poisoned Rita's well. She's sure it was Luke, but catching him is a problem. The sheriff will need to mark the well unsafe in case some thirsty stranger comes by. She has another well down by the barn for watering animals. We didn't take time to check that one, but it's too close to the barn for human use. It has a lot of seep water during rainy seasons."

Mr. Smith coughs and holds his chest. "The weather's been nice this week. I've been sitting out here most of the daylight hours. I haven't seen any strangers passing. Of course, after the shooting, Luke knows he's a wanted man. He wouldn't walk on the road."

Rita looks across the pasture past grazing cattle to where a warm breeze rustles yellow flowering weeds at the edge of the field. The Smiths' large collie trots close to Ben and George but runs into the barn as the boys ride on. The sounds of yelping puppies fill the air.

Mr. Smith chuckles. "My dog loves your boys, almost as much as her pups. She had four this time—two males and two females. They're pretty. I'll give you the first choice if you want one for the boys. One pup has taken to Ben and would follow him home if it could."

Rita glances at Doctor Tom and back at Mr. Smith. "I'll think about it, but right now, we have too much to worry about."

He nods. "I understand, but if you decide to let them have one, we'll keep it for you a few weeks until things settle down. We've come to love those boys like kinfolk, and let me tell you—they are hard workers. George can pitch hay like a man, and Ben tries his best, but he needs a little more height. Another year of growth should take care of his problem."

George slides off his horse first. "Mr. Smith, your big black cow, the one with the bent horn, has been staying off to herself since we went to check on the cows. Now she's trying to have her calf. Do you want me and Ben to stay out there and keep an eye on her?"

With a frown, Mr. Smith turns toward the doctor. "Doc, what do you suppose pulling a calf would do to me?"

Shaking his head, Doctor Tom says. "You know the answer to that question. I'd stay, but I need to get Rita home where she is not such an easy target. Do you want me to stop and see if Jacob Brown will come over and help?"

"He'll come over if you ask him, but I'm not on his good side. He was letting his cattle graze on my west meadow. I don't think he turned them in, but his fence is in sorry shape, and he didn't rush to get them out when I told him the first time. I had to threaten to start shooting before he got his cows. I wouldn't doubt them being in my meadow now. His pasture is eaten down to dust, and it's almost impossible to keep hungry cows inside a weak fence when there's grass on the other side. It's no problem since I plan to sell most of my herd, but I've already got him in a bad mood."

Rita looks toward the west. "It'll be a couple of hours until sunset. If Mrs. Smith doesn't mind, I can wait in the house with her, but Doctor, you and the boys need to get the picnic basket and eat your supper before going to pull a calf. That might take a long time."

Mrs. Smith stands and waves an arm. "All of you come inside. I have our supper waiting on the stove. We'll eat together. Then, Doctor Tom and the boys can go check on the cow. Anyway, she needs some time to try and have the calf on her own."

The Smith kitchen smells of apples and cinnamon. Two huge apple pies sit on the stove. "I planned to send one of those pies home with your boys. Instead, you can eat it here."

Mr. Smith leans back after supper and rubs his stomach. "Boys, if crooked horn has a healthy bull calf, I'll give it to you. She got over into Jacob's pasture in the spring and stayed a few days before I realized she was gone. Jacob Brown has a good looking black bull; I'm sure it is the daddy of her calf. She's one of my best cows, so a bull from those two should sire some excellent calves."

George grins. "Thank you, Mr. Smith, but we only have one heifer."

"Oh, don't worry. A bull calf will have to grow a couple of years. By then, hard-working boys like you should have several cows."

George looks at Rita and grins. "I hope so."

Mr. Smith stands. "I'll wait on the porch for you and let my supper settle."

The two boys jump up and grab their hats. Ben chuckles, "We better go see if we've got a bull calf. Doctor Tom, my horse is strong. We can ride double. A lot of fat men weigh more than both of us. I'll ride behind you."

By the time the dishes are washed, Rita hears her boys on the porch. "It's a bull, Mr. Smith, and a big one too. He's already up trying to get milk."

When Rita unlocks the door at Doctor Tom's house, Betty is sleeping, and Miss Pence is reading the newspaper. "Miss Pence, the doctor has gone to meet with the sheriff. He'll be here soon to take you home. I came back because someone put poison in my well. I'll need to have a new well drilled before I can live there."

"Oh, I'm sorry, Miss Rita. Someone was awful mean to do such a thing."

14 ~ Babies ~

O n a Sunday after church, Betty sits on the porch watching squirrels play while Rita gets the noon meal on the table. Helped by a cool breeze, leaves filter from the trees, and settle on the lawn. Betty tosses popcorn in the air, watching it float in the wind and land amid the new-fallen leaves. She giggles, pulling her sweater closed when a squirrel grabs a grain and runs up a tree.

The mocking bird has not been in the yard for several days. Rita thinks it has gone south for the winter and is glad Betty, in her clumsy condition, is not running to chase it away from the popcorn.

Rita notices that every few minutes, Betty frowns and hugs her stomach, but does not complain. Tossing a handful of popcorn onto the lawn, Betty giggles as two squirrels run to fill their mouths. A blue jay flies down to grab a piece. Betty stands and runs toward the bird, but trips and falls, hitting her head on a rock—part of a circle surrounding a flower bush.

The boys are getting ready to go check on Mr. Smith's cattle, and Doctor Tom is reading a book. Rita's scream calls them to the backyard.

Betty is unconscious, her head gushing blood. Rita gets a heavy quilt from the bedroom. Doctor Tom and the boys roll her onto the quilt and carry her into an examining room.

The sheriff walks into the office as they move her. "Poor girl. I hope she'll be okay."

George and Ben are standing in the hall with the sheriff when Rita steps from the room with the wet quilt on which they moved Betty. "Boys, I think you should go on to Mr. Smith's farm as soon as you eat your lunch. There is not a thing you can do to help Betty."

George nods, "Okay, we'll be back here before dark."

The sheriff steps back. "I'll go on to my office and get out of your way, but I want you to know my deputies are still watching this house."

"Thank you, Sheriff. We appreciate your concern."

Rita takes a washcloth and a pan of warm soapy water to bathe Betty. With a cold cloth, she washes the site where Betty's head hit the rock and places a clean bandage over it—with a thick dressing to absorb the blood, topped by a cold towel from the icebox to help impede the bleeding.

Betty moans and squeezes her stomach as contractions become strong.

Rita pats the cool cloth to Betty's cheeks. "Doctor Tom, several hours ago, I noticed her holding her stomach. She may have been having contractions for a long time."

Doctor Tom listens to the babies' heartbeats and shakes his head. "One is good, but I'm afraid one is getting weaker. It'll be God's will if they both make it. A baby has a lot of stress while coming into this world."

Hearing someone outside, Rita looks out the window. Ruth Parker's husband pulls into the yard. She opens the door as he jumps from the buggy. "Miss Rita, my wife needs the doc. Ruth's been having pains since this morning. The baby's coming."

"You'll have to bring her here. Betty fell, hit her head on a rock, and knocked herself unconscious."

"I don't know if I can move Ruth. Now, her pains are coming fast."

"You have to. Betty's in a bad way. Put Ruth in your buggy and drive her down here. She'll be fine. We'll put her in the second examining room."

He leaves the yard running his horses. Within fifteen minutes, Mr. Parker returns with Ruth. Her contractions are hard and close together. Rita and Mr. Parker get her onto a bed. Mr. Parker says, "Her water broke before we left home."

Rita hands him a cold cloth. "You can hold her hand and wash her face if you want, or you can go to the waiting room."

"I-I'll stay for a while."

Ruth's face is red, but Mr. Parker's face is ashen. Rita is afraid he may faint. "Mr. Parker, take the cloth with you and go sit in the waiting room for a while. I'll call if we need you." She watches as he stumbles to a couch.

Doctor Tom comes to Ruth's room. "Rita, go stay with Betty, she's getting close to delivery."

For the next two hours, they rush back and forth between the rooms. Ruth's baby comes first. Swallowing a lump in his throat, Doctor Tom says, "Ruth, you have a pretty baby. Rest while we get her cleaned up."

Almost breathless, Ruth calls, "Let me see. I want to hold my baby."

Doctor Tom ignores her pleas and calls Rita as he runs to his lab. "Take care of this baby while I help Betty."

Rita pats the baby, slaps its buttocks, and breathes into its mouth, but it is limp and without breath. Within seconds, the doctor brings another baby girl to the lab. She cries louder as he lays her in a bassinet.

Rita whispers with panic in her voice, "Doctor, Ruth's baby's not breathing!"

"He takes the little body and begins to work with it. Rita turns away to clean Betty's baby, put a diaper on it, and wrap it in a blanket."

Doctor Tom steps close to Rita and whispers. "Ruth's baby is dead. If Betty's baby is cleaned up, put it in Ruth's arms. Only you and I know this secret."

Rita nods and takes a crying baby to Ruth.

Doctor Tom puts the dead baby in a bassinet and returns to deliver Betty's second baby. He slaps the tiny twin on the buttocks to make it draw in a breath. The challenged young girl has given life to two babies, but within a short time, Betty breathes her last.

Looking into Betty's room, tears drizzle down Rita's face as she sees the pretty young girl at rest. "Lord, she deserves a beautiful place in heaven with you, and a new, perfect body. I can almost hear her saying 'pretty, pretty' as she touches a golden crown or feathery wing."

Before the crimson rays of sunset settle into black over the western mountains, the sheriff stops by to check on Betty.

Doctor Tom drops into a chair and motions to another one

nearby. He wipes at his eyes with a white handkerchief. "Sheriff, Betty had too many complications. Her blood pressure went too high. The pain in her head and the pain of childbirth was more than she could stand. Do you want to take a look at her head? It's a bad wound."

"No. No. I saw it when you put Betty in a room. I knew it was bad. Did her baby live?"

Doctor Tom takes a deep breath, sniffs, and again wipes at his eyes. "I did my best. It's too bad she couldn't have carried it another week or two."

"How about Ruth? She was almost full-term, wasn't she? She looked big enough to be carrying twins."

"She has two little girls. One is small, but with plenty of mother's milk, it may do fine. Ruth will make every effort possible to help them survive."

Rita closes the door to Ruth's room after placing the largest baby in Mr. Parker's arms. His face has regained its color along with a big smile. Sitting in a rocking chair beside Ruth's bed, he exclaims, "It's hard to believe we have twins. We've prayed for a baby for a long time, but God answered our prayers. He doubled them. Ruth, honey, the only day of my life happier than this was our wedding day." He bows his head as the baby clutches one of his huge fingers. "Dear God, thank you for these blessings. Help us to keep them safe."

Hearing the sheriff go out of the front door, Rita leaves the room and returns to join Doctor Tom in the kitchen. "Would you like me to make a fresh pot of coffee?"

He nods. "Rita, I would have been in trouble if you hadn't been here to help me with those babies and Betty. I'm going to miss her. The sheriff will contact the funeral home. They should be here later for Betty and the baby."

Putting the coffee pot on the stove to perk, Rita pulls out a chair across the table from the doctor. She sits, props her elbows on the table and squeezes her face in her hands for several seconds before folding her hands on the table and answering. "Yes, I'll miss her, but we know her spirit is with Jesus in heaven. She was an innocent child."

"Rita, even though Betty is gone, you and your boys have to stay here. You can't return to that farm without good well water, and with Luke trying to kill you."

"People in this town will talk."

"Those kinds of people don't matter."

"I don't want my boys hearing bad gossip about their mama."

"Those boys know what a good Christian woman you are, and they'll want you to stay safe."

"I know, but . . . ."

He reaches to wrap his hands over hers. "Rita, as soon as your divorce is final, will you marry me?"

Her mouth drops open, and her eyes go wide. "I-I, uh . . . ."

"Rita, I love you. Please don't think I'm asking because I need someone to cook and clean and be a nurse. I love you, and I want you for my wife. Also, I love your boys, and I want to call them ours. We can make a good life together."

She nods. "Yes."

"Rita, please say yes. I love you more than anything or anyone I've ever known."

She smiles. "I said, yes."

He jumps up and pulls her into his arms.

George and Ben stand inside the open door. "She said 'yes,' and we say yes." The four of them hug with the boys repeating, "Yes. Yes."

The coffee pot is about to boil over when Rita reaches to turn it off. She laughs, "Are you sure you didn't ask me because you like the way I make coffee?"

He pulls her back into his arms. "Your coffee is just a bonus."

Rita hears the door close as her boys leave the kitchen, but she does not move away from Tom's kiss until she hears Mr. Parker calling from the hallway.

Mr. Parker still wears a big smile. "Doctor Tom, and Miss Rita, I need to go home and feed my cows and horses. Will it be okay if Ruth stays here for the night? Miss Rita, I'll pay you to take care of her and the babies until I can hire a woman to come to our house and help."

"I'll be glad to take care of them. Mr. Parker, Doctor Tom asked me to be his wife as soon as a judge signs my divorce papers, but please don't tell anyone else. I'm a Christian woman. I don't want anyone accusing me of adultery."

"I won't say a thing about it. I heard Doc ask the question, and I'm pleased, but I've got plenty of happy news of my own to spread around town."

"Indeed, you do. Go on and feed your animals. I'll take care of Ruth and the babies. She will need to stay here for a few days until she regains some strength. Taking care of two babies takes a lot of energy."

"I'll ask around and try to find someone to help, and I've got to get to the store and buy things for another baby. We bought clothes for one, one cradle, and one baby bed. I'll see you in the morning."

Tiptoeing into Ruth's room, Rita sees both babies sleeping within Ruth's arms. Rita takes one and places it in the bassinet, and lays the other baby beside it. They wiggle as if trying to get closer.

Ruth opens her eyes and, for a second, looks frightened. "Rita, it's you. I thought someone had stolen my babies. Where are they?"

"On the left side of your bed. You need to rest now. Both babies are in one bassinet. Twin babies like to be close."

"You seem to know a lot about babies."

"I raised two, and I read about health issues at every opportunity. Doctor Tom gave me a textbook for nurses. It has three chapters on babies."

"Did Betty have her baby?"

"Yes, but it was too young."

"Oh. I'm so sorry. How is Betty?"

"She didn't survive. She fell, hit her head on a rock, and her blood pressure went too high."

"Poor girl, she had a rough life. When will they have her funeral?"

"I imagine tomorrow. The sheriff will take care of the arrangements."

"I remember when my first twin was born, but when the second twin arrived, I didn't know anything. The shot Doctor Tom gave me must have kicked in before the hard labor started for the second one."

"The first twin stretches the birth canal, so the second one followed easier."

"I didn't know I was having twins until I discovered two babies in my arms."

"Doctor Tom didn't want to stress you, so he didn't mention twins. The small one had a weaker heartbeat, but Tom said it's strong now. He thinks, with your love and good care, they will both be fine and grow into beautiful, healthy young ladies."

"Oh, I hope so. I love my babies so much."

"The doctor thinks you should have plenty of milk for both of them, but if not, you can supplement with goat's milk."

"Our neighbors have several goats. They drink the milk and make cheese with it. They've offered it to us on numerous occasions."

"Ruth, you need to get some sleep. You'll be awake several times during the night with the babies. I'll move a cot in here so I can nap in between helping you. Call me if you want or need anything. You shouldn't get up without help. You might faint and hurt yourself or one of the twins."

"I'm not prone to fainting. I can take care of my babies."

Shaking her head, Rita is firm when she says, "Women who have never fainted in their life often pass out cold the first days after having a baby. Don't try to get up unless I'm awake to hold on to you.

Okay? I need you to promise."

Ruth smiles a weak smile. "I promise, but I hate to bother you."

Rita grins. "The doctor pays me to help his patients. In the morning, you can walk into the kitchen if you feel strong enough to move about, but not tonight. Both babies will need fresh diapers, maybe gowns, and their bed changed. Also, I've boiled water. It's cooling now, but during the night, I'll need to warm it to body temperature before they can drink it. Tomorrow your milk should come in, and you can nurse them, but they will still need a little water between feedings."

Ruth smiles and closes her eyes. "Rita, thank you for helping me. I'm so happy with my babies. I almost feel as if I could get up and dance, but I'll do as you say and be careful."

15 ~ Kidnapped

George and Ben step through the back door, and Ben calls, "Mama, what's for supper?"

George doesn't give her a chance to answer before he interrupts. "You should see our new calf. He's already running around with the other calves and is as big as some of the older ones. We named him Champ. I wish we had papers on him. I think he could be a champion."

He takes a cookie from a cloth-covered plate, breaks off half, and hands it to Ben. Looking at Rita, he asks, "How's Betty? Did she have her baby?"

"Ruth Parker's husband brought Ruth into the office. They have two beautiful little girls." Looking away from a simmering pot, Rita places a hand on his shoulder. "George, Betty died. The sheriff and the undertaker took her and the baby to the funeral home. Her blood pressure went too high after she fell. Her funeral will be tomorrow afternoon."

Ben shakes his head and runs his fingers over a long healing scratch on his arm. "I don't need to go. I'll stay at school." He frowns and looks up at Rita, "I should have been nicer to her, but she was always trying to hug me. I don't like girls hugging on me."

George stares at Rita as if he is in shock. "Dead! The baby too. I didn't think she would die. Poor Betty. God took her to heaven—don't you think? She was as good as she knew how to be."

He drops onto a chair and stares at his hands. "As you said, Mama, she was just a baby in a big girl's body." Looking up he asks, "What time is the funeral?"

"It's at the church at two-thirty."

"If you'll write a note for my teacher, I'll leave at two and walk over. Ben, you can walk with me if you want."

"No." Ben waves his hand. "She won't know if I'm there or not. Besides, I'm only a kid. I don't need to go—do I, Mama?"

Rita shakes her head. "No. You don't need to go. The sheriff doesn't want me, or you boys to go. He thinks it's dangerous for us. Since a wooded area is so near the cemetery, someone could shoot at us and lose themselves in the woods, or travel miles down the river before deputies could get on the trail."

"It's a long way to the river."

"Through those woods, the creek is not far, and it leads to the Arkansas River. A small flat bottom boat could reach the river quicker than men on horses. He might have plans to pick up a bigger boat at the junction. Boys, I don't want to frighten you for no reason, but you must be careful. I believe Luke's insane."

She hugs herself and rubs her arms as if she is freezing. "Doctor Tom plans to go, but I'll stay here to take care of Ruth and her twins. I think you boys should go to school as usual. No one will expect you to attend the funeral. Or, if you want, you can stay here with me. I'll keep a gun close."

George stands and puts an arm around Rita's shoulders. "Mama, I want you to know we love you as much as boys can love their mama, and we're sorry you had to tolerate the mean things Pa did."

Ben stands with him and puts an arm around her. "Yeah, Mama, It's too bad that Pa wasn't a good man like Grandpa, Doctor Tom, or Mr. Smith."

"Yes. I don't know what makes some people mean, but I'm glad you are like my Pa. He was a good Christian man." She opens the oven door to remove a pan of cornbread.

"Boys, get yourselves a plate and dish up some ham, beans, and fried potatoes. I didn't have time to do much cooking today, but I prepared the cornbread and potatoes fresh. I'll fix a plate for Ruth. Doctor Tom may be late. He went with the sheriff to make funeral plans."

Ben grabs a plate, fills it, and eats fast. "Hurry George, it'll be dark soon, and we didn't feed our calf before going to check on Mr. Smith's cows." He crams a bite of cornbread crust in his mouth, sets his plate in the sink, and gets a bucket of water for mixing the calf's milk.

"George, I'm going on to mix the milk while this water's warm. Hurry up. We'll need to feed Dolly too. Doctor Tom went with the sheriff in his official car. You know how that man likes to talk. They'll be late, for sure."

Gulping his milk after eating another cookie, George takes a few minutes to step into Ruth's room and look at her sleeping babies before he rushes out the door.

Rita dunks his plate in soapy dishwater and leans against the window facing to watch as her oldest boy jogs toward the barn.

Hearing Ruth call, she hurries away to help.

"Rita, I hated to call you, but I've finished my supper and don't know what to do with the plate."

"No problem, I'll take it." She glances at the babies. "They look so sweet, snuggled together in that little bed."

The kitchen door slams, and George yells, "Mama!"

Leaving the room, Rita pulls on the door. Whispering as she enters the kitchen, "Not so loud, George. You'll disturb the babies."

"Mama, Ben's gone! The calf milk is spilled across the pen, and the pitchfork we use for Dolly's hay has blood on it."

Rita slaps a hand over her mouth as a moan escapes. "Run to the sheriff's house and get someone over here, quick. Quick!"

Grabbing a shortened broomstick from the window sill, George leaves, letting the door slam. He jumps off the porch, running.

Wringing her hands, Rita drops into a chair and bows her head to pray.

Doctor Tom rushes in the door. "Rita, the sheriff and two deputies are at the barn. They'll find him. Ben's a smart kid. He'll be okay. The sheriff told me to stay here with you. Go to the waiting room where the only low window has heavy drapes. From outside, no one can see us in there. Get the gun from my desk, and make sure it's loaded. I'll get the one in my bedroom."

"I need to explain what's going on to Ruth."

"Okay, the windows in the patient rooms are high so no one can see inside, but don't turn on any bright lights to attract attention. Close her door when you leave."

Throughout the night, Rita hears people in the street and yard.

She takes care of Ruth and the babies, warming water bottles without turning on bright lights. In the dim glow from a lamp, she changes diapers and baby gowns, rocking one baby while Ruth holds a water bottle for the other—all the while she prays for her boys, for Doctor Tom, and the safety of those searching for Ben.

The sun is threatening to wake the world with rose-colored warmth when someone knocks on the door. Rita places a sleeping baby in the bassinet and rushes to stand beside Doctor Tom as a man tells them deputies found signs where a man and boy walked along the creek to its junction with the Arkansas River.

"We could tell the man had a boat concealed in the brush beside the river. With some difficulty, he pulled it out to escape. They could be headed for the Mississippi River, maybe on to New Orleans or another good-sized town. We've alerted every county and town between here and the ocean to be on the lookout for them. We found a man's blue shirt resting on weeds beside the river. It had blood smeared down the sleeve and almost a full-size bloody handprint on the front. He must have dropped the shirt as he struggled to get the boat from the weeds and into the current."

Rita nods. "That's probably Luke's. The evening someone tried to break in our farmhouse window, the man watching the house from the meadow had on a blue shirt."

"We think the boy stuck a pitchfork in the man's shoulder. A pitchfork is not the cleanest instrument around. He'll be looking for a doctor within a few days."

Rita gasps, "Oh, I hope Ben is not injured. Tetanus germs are around barnyards."

Shaking his head, the deputy turns to Rita. "It wasn't the boy's blood. The shirt had a hole in it from the pitchfork."

Gritting her teeth, Rita nods, "Ben's always been a fighter."

"Your other son is blaming himself for not getting to the barn in time to help his brother. For a second, I thought George might jump in and start swimming downriver, but I put a hand on his arm, and he stepped away."

Frowning, Rita asks, "What are the sheriff's plans for catching them?"

"He knows someone with a boat big enough to run the river. He's gone over there now trying to make arrangements to rent it. We'll do our best to keep you posted on what's going on." He steps out, pulling the door closed behind him.

Doctor Tom paces the floor. "I feel useless here. I should be looking for Ben, but the sheriff insisted I stay here to protect you."

Straightening her body, Rita snaps, "I have a gun. I can take care of myself. Go with the men to find Ben. I'll shoot Luke if he steps a foot in here."

Doctor Tom stares at her for a second before turning to put a hand on the doorknob.

Rita wraps her arms around him. "Bring my boy back to me. Please! And stay safe. I need you as well." She steps away, sobbing.

"I'll do my best. Keep the doors locked, and remember I love you and the boys."

Before she can answer, the door closes behind him.

All-day, Rita keeps herself busy taking care of Ruth and the babies and praying. She even shells and cans a basket of peas left in the doctor's basement. The preacher stops by after Betty's funeral to tell her that most of the town attended and brought flowers from their yards and gardens.

George's face seems locked in a frown since Ben disappeared. He continues to take care of Mr. Smith's cattle and the calves belonging to Ben and himself. Mr. Smith began teaching him to shoot the day after Ben vanished. He gave George a pistol to wear on his hip and plenty of ammunition. He can't wear the gun to school, but otherwise, he wears it during daylight hours and practices with Mr. Smith watching.

In the following days, Rita notices how George hides his emotions, except for his perpetual frown. He talks very little. He tells her of his work with Mr. Smith, but nothing of school and friends.

One day George tells Rita that Mr. Smith gave him a lariat rope and a long bullwhip and said, "George, a lariat is something every cowboy needs from time to time. I've only had a real use for this bullwhip once in my life, but it's not a bad thing if you know how to use it. Hang it in the barn and play with it when you have time. Someday, I'll teach you its benefits and how to control it. First, you need to get good with a gun and lariat."

A week goes by before the sheriff, his deputy, and Doctor Tom return. They found no trace of Ben and Luke after they entered the river. People in the river towns averted their eyes and claimed they hadn't seen a boat with a man and a boy, but an old doctor near New Orleans said he treated a puncture wound in a man's shoulder. He was confident it looked like a pitchfork made it. He suggested we call in the Feds to investigate and said several people within the last few years had reported boys missing. The local sheriff seemed irritated at the doctor and said, "Old man, quit blowing smoke and mind your own business. Those boys were runaways and vagrants. I don't want them hanging around our town."

The sheriff taps his boot against the wood floor in the hall. "Rita, don't give up. Keep praying. I'm going to the Feds with this, and I'll not quit until I find Ben, but keep quiet about it. I think someone in this town is feeding information to Luke. Do you remember anyone around here who was his friend, or maybe someone related to him?"

She shakes her head. "As far as I know, all his relatives are in Louisiana, the southern part. One time he told me his kinfolk owned a peninsula surrounded by alligators. They hunted gators, fished, and raised a few crops for money until they discovered easier ways. He laughed and said it was easier and more profitable to take what they wanted and make runaways work for them than to muck around in those black bottomlands. He thought it funny when telling that lawmen snooping around helped to fatten the alligators."

"He doesn't sound like someone you could fall for."

"I was fourteen and isolated on Pa's farm after Mama died. I was young, ignorant in the ways of the world, and eager to talk to anyone stopping by." She leans her head forward with a hand over her face. "As Luke said, he was used to taking what he wanted and . . . Pa made me marry him. That's the only bad thing I associate with Pa, but he believed it was the right thing to do."

Taking a deep breath, she continues. "I thought most of Luke's talk was lies and brag, but when I asked why he didn't stay in Louisiana, he shrugged and admitted he got a little too ambitious, and his cousins ran him off."

The sheriff reaches for the doorknob. "Think hard, and if you remember anyone, let me know."

A chill runs through her neck and down her back. "Sheriff, do you think he could have been telling the truth about captured runaways? Luke had very few, if any, decent morals. He liked to gamble, and he hung around with other lazy bums. Pete Omak was one's name. Maybe the Feds can get some information from him. He's a low-life like Luke."

"I don't know, Rita. The bones of missing law enforcement officers should have been found within the last thirteen years."

She nods. "You would think so, but not if they were in the river or those Louisiana swamps. Oh, I pray that he didn't leave Ben in a swamp with alligators?"

Rita goes through her days—like a zombie—cooking, cleaning, and helping Doctor Tom. After Ruth goes home with the twins, Rita bakes more and takes food to some of Doctor Tom's patients. She never stays to visit, just long enough to pray and ask them to continue praying for Ben.

Every good deed, Rita performs increases her admirers, and people begin to form prayer groups. Even men playing checkers at the general store start and end their sessions with prayers for Ben.

The sheriff sends Ben's school picture to every town

newspaper operating near the Mississippi River along the borders of Arkansas, Louisiana, and Mississippi. He receives several letters from people thinking they have seen a boy fitting Ben's description. He gives the messages to the federal officers.

On a Tuesday morning, Doctor Tom asks Rita to pack him a sack lunch. "I'm going over to the military base at Jacksonville and ask them to watch when they fly training missions over southern Louisiana, and to take notice of any farms looking as if they have young boys working with patrolling guards."

"Are civilians allowed on that base? I'm afraid they may run you off before you get through the gate."

"Camp Pike is not as restricted as it was during the war. I went to school with one of the camp doctors. I wrote to him about our situation, and he invited me for a visit. He'll try to get me in to see the commander. It's a long shot, but we need to try everything we can."

"Louisiana is a long way for them to go."

"I've heard they fly training missions all over the south. They won't organize a mission totally for us. Still, maybe they can make a few low swipes over peninsulas when they happen to be in the Southern Louisiana area, and give the location of any suspicious-looking spots to the FBI."

One day, two men from the FBI stop to talk with Rita. They want her to tell them everything she remembers Luke saying that could have anything to do with captured runaways. They have heard other stories over the last ten years, and they seem to point to disappearing boys.

Rita tries to remember the bragging Luke did. None of it was good. He grew up in an evil environment, even his mama did her best to cheat people, but Rita tries hard to piece every story together. An almost unbelievable group of horror tales result. Things that, at that time, she thought were stories he made up to impress her of how tough he was—and details that she, a Christian girl, did her best to forget.

Before the investigators leave, Rita asks them if they have talked to the local law enforcement in Louisiana about the boys.

"That local sheriff didn't seem to have an interest in finding missing boys. Your sheriff said he seemed irritated at an old doctor down there that tried to provide information and said, 'Old man, quit blowing smoke and mind your own business. Those boys were runaways and vagrants. I don't want them hanging around our town.'"

Rita frowns. "I think any sheriff should want to help return boys to their homes, instead of running them out of town."

"That sheriff was gone the day we were there, but we talked to the doctor. His thoughts were the same as yours. We have a file on the Louisiana sheriff, and he's under investigation. It will not go well for him if he's taken part in the kidnapping and holding young boys against their will."

The Doctor's Luck

16 ~ A Fight

One afternoon George comes home from school with a torn shirt, a swollen eye, and bruised knuckles. Rita grabs his arm, "What happened to you?"

He turns away. "Nothing much. I had a little fight."

"Why? I thought all the boys were your friends."

"Most of them, but one keeps making nasty remarks about Ben. Today, I busted his mouth. He'll be quiet for a while."

"Who is it?"

"It doesn't matter. I don't think he'll say anything else. Right now, his lip is bigger than his brain."

"It matter's to me. What is his name?"

"Bobby Omak. He's a bully. Mom, I try to ignore him, but today he pushed me too far. He's the same kid that tripped Ben last year. Ben is half his size, but Bobby was ready to run before that round was over."

George steps toward the door. "Some bums don't know when to stop prodding."

Rita frowns and turns off a burner under a pot on the stove. "I want to hear the complete story, from beginning to end. The exact words."

"I don't have time. That fight made me late. I have to go feed Mr. Smith's cattle."

She shakes her head. "All right, tell me what he said to start it while I get you a cold cloth to wash your face."

"Oh, Mama." George sighs, takes the cloth from Rita's hand and slaps it against his face. "Ouch, my cheek caught a fist."

"George, I'm waiting, and your eye looks bad. It looks like more than a little fight to me."

"Okay. Okay. Bobby said, 'Your skinny worm of a brother is probably gator shit on the banks of the Mississippi River by now.'"

"George! Such language!"

George shrugs. "You said to tell you his exact words. That's what I did. He didn't say anything after that because I busted his mouth with my right hand, blacked his eye with my left, and swung several punches to his middle. I admit he hit me a few times, but he's been needling me all week. I had all I could take."

"What has he been saying all week?"

George stomps his foot into a boot. "Mama, I've got to go. I'll tell you more after supper."

Rita frowns and nods.

Stomping his foot into the second boot, he says. "He's been telling me that he wants to teach me to play cards. He said, his pa got most of his farm equipment from playing cards with Pa, but he needs a few more things."

Rita squeezes her eyes shut and shakes her head. "I figured that's where my pa's farm equipment went and my animals too."

Opening the door to leave, George turns to hug Rita. "I have the best Mama, but a sorry Pa. And you don't have to worry about me playing cards with Bobby Omak. I don't want to learn anything from him."

"Be careful on the farm. I'll have supper ready when you get home." Rita pats his shoulder.

"Mama, we were away from the school grounds when the fight started, so don't worry about the teacher or a call from the school board." He leaves on the run.

Sliding a chair away from the kitchen table, Rita sits, folds her arms at her waist, and fights the angry emotions running through her head. *Luke was, is, and may always be a thief, liar, and one of the worst of sinners. He took animals and equipment that belonged to me. He sold those things or gambled them away without a care that I would need them to survive and take care of our children.*

Bowing her head onto arms resting on the table, Rita prays, "Dear God, I am grateful for all the blessings you have given me, but please watch over my boys and keep them safe, above all watch over Ben, while he is away from home. Lord, keep Tom and all the men searching for Ben within your secure protection. In Jesus' name, I pray. And, Lord, use your wisdom to handle Luke. I can't bring myself to pray for him. Amen.

Feeling the urge to help someone, Rita takes a large mixing bowl from the cabinet to mix a batch of cookies for the people that pray for Ben and for those that are struggling with hard times caused by the depression.

The Doctor's Luck

17~ Missing Boys

A month passes with no more contact from the FBI or the pilots at Camp Pike. Rita continues to pray for Ben as she goes about her work, and as she bakes cookies and muffins for the elderly and disabled people in the community. They tell her they have not, and will not give up praying for Ben until he comes home.

Boys from George's Sunday Bible Class meet at the farm every Sunday afternoon and draw water from the poisoned well and pour it in the garden. After a while, they stop seeing poison residue in the bucket, but the young men are having fun and continue to gather each week. The basket of cookies that Rita sends for them to eat helps encourage and remind them of the need to keep praying. One Sunday afternoon, when George comes home to get ready to go feed Mr. Smith's cattle, he tells Rita that he asked the boys not to return to the farm until Ben is home to go with them. "Mama, we always pray before eating, but I feel guilty for laughing and having fun when I know Ben must be suffering."

"Son, I know how you feel, but laughing and being with your friends is a benefit to your health. Everyone I know is praying for Ben. That's all we can do. God will help us to find him, and God will not be angry with you for having fun with your friends."

Pausing, Rita looks up. "In the Old Testament, Ecclesiastes 3:4, it states, *There is...a time to weep and a time to laugh, a time to mourn and a time to dance . . . .* When Ben comes home, he'll want to go with you and your friends. Don't mourn when it's not a time for it. Ben will come home—have faith and keep praying."

At last, Doctor Tom can pay his overdue bills. With a smile, he places Rita's wages on the kitchen table. "Now, you can buy a new dress."

She wants to smile, but tears fill her eyes. "I'm managing, but I'll get a new dress after I take care of a few necessities."

Doctor Tom shakes his head. "Rita, you are one of a kind, always thinking of someone else instead of your own needs."

With money in front of her, Rita sits down with a Sears Roebuck Catalogue and orders George two shirts, socks, underwear, and two pairs of blue jeans. She hides the rest of her money and tells Doctor Tom she will repay him for her taxes as soon as she saves enough.

Almost everyone, including Rita, is afraid to trust banks after the banks failed and people lost money during the Great Depression. The money she saved to pay property taxes on her farm was lost. Now, her savings rest in an old baking powder can at the back of the doctor's pantry. She fills out a second order for Ben some new clothes but tucks it inside the can with her savings.

After weeks of waiting, Rita receives a notice to meet with the lawyer concerning her divorce. Doctor Tom locks his house and places a note on the front door, saying he will be in the office after one. In the doctor's buggy with Dolly trotting, Rita is on the way to

Conway as soon as the boys leave for school.

The judge signs Rita's divorce decree giving her total custody of George and Ben and declares her sole owner of the farm. A tiny smile is on her lips as she holds the legal papers. "Now Luke can never take Pa's land. Even if he kills me, it will go to my boys."

Doctor Tom buys Rita an engagement ring while they are in town. Tom wants to get married right away, but Rita tells him, "I love you, and I'll wear your ring, but we have to wait until Ben comes home for the wedding."

"Rita, I understand that you are overwhelmed with stress over Ben, but don't forget I love you and the boys. We're in this struggle together."

With her head lowered and her hands clenched tight, she answers, "I haven't forgotten. I love you more than ever for waiting and for your help, but I can't celebrate our love until Ben comes home."

Mr. Smith agrees to give George one calf a month, during the winter, for his work of taking care of the Smith cattle. George thinks that is a grand deal, until after a hard freeze when all the animals need hay, every day. It is past dark each evening before he arrives back at the doctor's house.

One bitter cold evening, while Doctor Tom works late, and after Rita cooks supper, she leaves it sitting on the stove and goes to feed the calf and Doctor Tom's horse. The sky is spitting snow and light sleet as she leaves the house imagining George with his hat pulled low, riding Mr. Smith's horse through an icy wind that cuts near to the bone. She is sure when seeing the fat calf snuggled in straw close to Dolly's stall with the mare munching hay, George will know Rita has fed them. And after rubbing down Mr. Smith's horse and giving it grain and hay, George will rush inside where a hot supper waits.

She was right. George plops onto a chair near the warm oven. "Mama, you shouldn't have gone to the barn by yourself. It was a nice motherly thing to do, but don't do it again. Pa wants to kill you more than Ben or me. I have Mr. Smith's gun, and he's taught me well. I watch for Pa as I watch for rattlers on a summer day. I won't let him take me."

She gasps. "George, could you shoot your own pa?"

His jaw tightens, and his eyes compress to narrow slits. "Just as fast as a big rattler. He's the reason Ben's gone, and he tried to poison us all. You know he was mean to Ben and me when we were little boys. Remember the time he beat Ben for waking him from his drunken nap? Ben was four years old. Since then, I've hated the demon that could do such an awful thing to a little kid."

"George! You shock me. I've tried to teach you not to hate."

"Mama, I wouldn't shoot him for no reason, but I'll defend myself and anyone else needing protection."

Taking a deep breath, Rita turns and stirs a pot on the stove.

Rubbing his hands together, George holds them near the oven door. "It sure was cold today. One of Mr. Smith's cows decided to have her calf this afternoon. It was so cold I thought about giving up on finding her, but I don't want anyone to give up on finding Ben."

Moving away from the stove, he continues. "I knew the cow

would try to hide in the warmest place available. Sure enough, Blackie was in a thicket of small cedars. The wind within the thicket wasn't bad." He lifts a piece of green cedar from his pant leg and flicks it into the trash can.

"Those trees and bushes were close together, almost like a wall. After I helped her with the calf, I left them there. I figure it was as warm there as inside a barn, and that baby didn't need to walk through the cold wind.

"It's a pretty black and white heifer calf, but it was almost too big for that young cow. I had to help her; then I lifted, rubbed, and patted the calf until it stood up. The cow was licking her baby when I left. I'm sure glad I didn't give up and come home. They both might have died without help."

"Son, you've turned into quite a cowboy." Rita pats his shoulder.

"I would love it if Ben was here with me. Mama, I pray for him all day long. Do you think God's already taken him?"

With a lurch, Rita turns to clean the sink. Tears sting her eyes, and she swallows a lump in her throat. "No, son. I believe Ben is alive. Keep praying. You know what a fighter Ben is. He won't give up. One of these days he'll come home."

"Yeah. Ben will fight to the end. Even the older kids at school didn't want to tangle with him, because he wouldn't give up in a fight."

More and more, Rita assists Doctor Tom with patients. Several of the older women request Rita to massage their aching spines and shoulders. They don't want to expose themselves to a man, even if he is a kind medical doctor. However, Doctor Tom stays busy with patients truly needing his help. Word of his talents and kind heart travel throughout the county and more patients come to him. Many of them cannot pay, but that does not deter him from helping.

The week before Thanksgiving, a detective from the FBI knocks on the door. He tells Rita they discovered a farm where they think several young men and boys were held hostage. The day before the planned raid on the farm, the prisoners revolted. Pilots from Fort Pike noticed the farm on a peninsula surrounded by large alligators, but when pilots flew military helicopters in, they found a couple of dead men. Evidence showed their attackers were wielding large sharp boards, the kind of flat sharpened boards used to knock the leaves off sugar cane, and they hit vital spots on the guard's necks.

Investigation revealed it was not a legal prison camp. Young captives were forced to stay and work. Anyone trying to leave on the narrow road without defensive weapons would be attacked and killed by the alligators.

The military dropped small bombs into the water, causing the gators to disappear into the deep. About every three hundred feet beside the road, they found a dead alligator riddled with rifle bullets.

"A surprise attack by prisoners killed the guards before they could shoot any of the boys. We think the young men frightened most of the alligators into the deep by firing shots at those on the road with guns they took from the guards."

The FBI detective, standing on the steps in the warm sun, clears his throat and requests a drink of water.

"Yes. Of course. Please forgive my poor manners. Come on in and have a seat while I get you a drink." Rita hands him a glass of water and waits for him to drink before asking, "Where are the boys? It was warm when Ben disappeared. He'll freeze trying to walk home in this weather without a coat."

The man shakes his head. "We don't know where they went. Footprints are beside the river, but the trail ends there. The boat that, we think, took Ben to Louisiana was left beside the river. We estimate the safe capacity of the boat to be around twenty skinny boys, but the helicopter pilot estimated around fifty boys were in the field when he flew over."

Rita sinks into a chair. "Please, God, not drownings from an overcrowded boat."

"We haven't found any bodies along the river. Although gators are numerous in that section of the river."

Gasping, Rita grabs a wet dishtowel from the sink and runs it over her face before sinking back onto her chair.

"Miss Rita, are you okay? You look mighty pale."

Compressing her lips, Rita nods. "I'll be fine."

The young man continues, "My captain thinks one of the boys drove the boat up the river with around twenty-five at a time dropping them off at intervals, maybe a mile apart, near the shore so they wouldn't attract attention. He thinks the last twenty-five came to Arkansas and continued northwest along the river. The Arkansas National Guard found the abandoned boat, out of gas, a few miles south of Conway. Your county sheriff and his deputies are searching the area."

"Oh, I pray they all escaped safe and sound, and I hope the FBI catches every man, or woman, who helped to capture and mistreat those kids."

"So far, we haven't caught a one, but we are working at it. Our goal is the same as yours."

Rita stands, her hands shaking and her voice quivering. "Sir, stay and share our midday meal if you have time. For a windy day like this, I made a pot pie with carrots, peas, and plenty of potatoes and chicken."

"That sounds delicious if you have enough to share."

"Yes. We do." She nods and opens the oven to check the pie.

"Is that a chocolate cake beside the pie?

"Yes. It's a simple cake. I punch holes and pour fudge sauce over it. It was easy to prepare for a busy morning."

"My mama used to make those for me. Nothing is better on a cold day than chicken pot pie and a fudge drizzled cake."

Rita smiles, "Bring my boy home, and I'll make you a dozen fudge soaked cakes."

"I'll do my best, with or without the cake, but a fudge cake to share with my buddies would be appreciated." He bends and turns his head sideways to look in the oven as she removes the chicken pot pie.

Doctor Tom rushes into the kitchen and nods a greeting to the detective. "I can't stop to sit and eat. I have three patients waiting— one needs emergency stitches. Rita, if you'll serve me a plate and let it cool a little, I'll come back and grab a few bites after I stitch up the boy's hand." He rushes away, leaving Rita with the FBI detective.

The man continues to give Rita information as they eat lunch. "I neglected to tell you we think at least one girl is with the group. We found a pink ribbon and a comb near one of the dead guards. Defending her may be a reason for the revolt, especially if she's a sister or sweetheart of one of the young prisoners."

She nods. "I understand. I'm sure either one of my boys would risk their lives to defend the other. They've had some awful fights, but they'd stand side by side against anyone else."

"That's the way brothers are, and it works the same with a sister."

"Does the doctor have a telephone?"

Shaking her head, she says, "Not yet. It's taken a long time to get service out here, but he's supposed to get one installed next week."

"We'll send messages to you by the sheriff. Don't give information to anyone but the sheriff, or a well-known deputy. We still think someone is informing the gang of cutthroats of our movements."

Gripping a potholder, Rita asks, "Has anyone seen or heard from Luke?"

"I don't know of any contacts."

"He's evil. Watch your step around him. Drop by anytime. I appreciate the work the FBI is doing to help my boy and the others."

"I'll do it. Thank you for sharing that delicious meal." He grins, "I won't forget about your fudge-cake, although I can't take one to share with my friends, my boss frowns on anyone taking gifts or bribes as he calls it. But thanks for the offer." He starts down the steps, but turns fast, "Oh, for your information, we are still investigating that Louisiana sheriff."

18 ~ Reunion

More cold weather blows in from the northwest, bringing an overcast sky with thick clouds loaded with snow. Rita rushes as if she is on a limited schedule to complete her work. She peers out every window she passes, searching to the horizon for the shape of a young man, but none appears.

George runs inside after school, takes a mouthful of the sandwich Rita has prepared for him, and hurries to his bedroom to change into work clothes and strap on Mr. Smith's gun. Before leaving, he gulps a cup of warm potato soup. "Mama, this is good. If I ever marry, I hope my wife can cook as well as you." Stuffing the wax paper wrapped sandwich in a coat pocket, he opens the kitchen door. "I'll eat my sandwich on the way."

"George, if it starts to snow hard before you leave, stay for the night. I'll worry about you, but if you promise to remain at the Smith farm, I won't agonize as much as if I thought you were on your way home in a blizzard."

Stepping back into the kitchen and pulling the door closed against the freezing wind, he turns to stare at her. "I can't simply blurt out that I'm spending the night."

"Ask if it's all right for you to sleep in the hayloft. Mrs. Smith will invite you inside the house. If not, you'll be warm in the hay with a couple of horse blankets spread over you. Promise you'll stay if it's snowing hard? Doctor Tom, or I will feed your calf."

153

"Okay, I'll do it." He leaves the porch running toward the barn to saddle Mr. Smith's horse.

Doctor Tom left in the afternoon to deliver a baby for a young woman who is almost two weeks overdue. It is her first child, and he expects to be there several hours—maybe all night.

Rita keeps busy with household chores, removing a pan of soup from the burner, and preparing the coffee pot, so it is ready to put over a flame when the doctor gets home. Snow is falling fast before she gets her boots on, a gun in her pocket, and a bucket of warm water ready for mixing the calf milk.

She makes her way into the barn without spilling the water. Glancing around, she hastens to the shelf holding the powdered milk. With a large wooden spoon, Rita measures and stirs the milk. Hooking the milk bucket on a rail of the calf's stall, she steps back. The hungry calf latches onto the rubber milk teat with gusto.

With her face tilted toward the floor, Rita's eyes search the barn. Her ears are keen for hearing the smallest sound, separate from the loud slurping of the calf. A cascade of dust filters from the hayloft, glittering in the lantern light. Trying not to let the intruder know she is aware of someone in the loft, she talks to the calf as if it were a human baby. "I'll get you some hay and a fresh bucket of water for your tub. Easy now, Baby, don't knock your bucket off the rail."

Picking up the water bucket, she walks to the door and with composure steps outside. Running as fast as she can in the snow, she makes it into the house and locks the door behind her. She has barely caught her breath when she hears Doctor Tom's horse and buggy coming down the street, with the bell on Dolly's collar jingling.

Rita races out the front door and down the walk to meet the doctor, almost sliding into the moving buggy. "Tom, someone's in our hayloft. Get the sheriff. Hurry!" She does not wait for an answer, but runs to the house, slamming the door behind her.

Looking from the kitchen window, Rita sees George on Mr. Smith's horse heading for the barn. She steps onto the back porch. "George! George! Come here."

George has a long, wool scarf tied over his hat and ears. The whistling wind and rustle of dry leaves in nearby pin oak trees impede Rita's words. Warm leather gloves keep his hands warm while twirling a rope beside the horse. The lariat holds his undivided attention as he rides into the barn.

A gun roars. Rita jumps from the porch. Her feet soar over the snow as if she were riding a magic carpet. Doctor Tom's pistol is tight in her hand.

In the center of the barn, Luke stands with her pa's revolver pointed at George. Within the next few seconds, Luke is on the floor, bleeding. Rita picks up her pa's gun and drops it in her pocket. George is tying Luke up for the sheriff.

Luke whines, "Rita, I fired a warning shot. I wouldn't hurt my boy."

Standing in front of Luke, Rita demands, "Where is Ben? What did you do with Ben?"

"I don't know. I didn't do anything with Ben."

"You're a liar!" Rita kicks his head, bumping it against a nearby post. Her hand quivers with the weight of the gun, but she continues to point it at Luke. "I'm tempted to eliminate you from God's earth." She is still pointing Doctor Tom's gun at Luke when the sheriff parks his car near the barn door. Doctor Tom is close behind with Dolly and the buggy.

"Sheriff, Luke was threatening George with my pa's gun—I shot him in the shoulder." She hands both guns to the doctor and drops down on a nail keg. "He says he doesn't know Ben's location." She covers her face with her hands and sobs, her body shaking as she cries.

The sheriff grabs Luke, snaps a pair of handcuffs over the thin rope George used, and drags him toward the car. "I believe he'll talk to me."

Before the sheriff can drive away, Ben runs into the barn and into his mama's arms. George puts his arms around them both, and Doctor Tom hugs all three. A stranger could not tell if they are laughing or crying, but the sheriff knows the moisture, on their cheeks, denotes a happy group.

A teenage boy and girl appear in the doorway. "Hey, everyone, meet my friends Pedro and Lenita. Pedro helped to save us." Ben points at Luke. "Sheriff, my pa captured and sold me as a slave. George, he intended to get you, but I came along first. They would have paid five hundred for you, but I wasn't big enough—he only got two hundred for me. Sheriff, can you beat that two hundred out of him, or find an alligator pond and feed him to the gators? They kept threatening to throw all of us in that murky water with the gators."

The sheriff laughs. "I think not, but before he escapes this problem, he'll wish he'd never got his hands on you. The FBI will want you and your friends to testify. They should be here tomorrow."

Rita and Doctor Tom lead George, Ben, Pedro, and Lenita into the house. Ben and the new friends are starving. They found a tree with a few pears near where they dropped one of the boys from the boat. In another location, they picked up some pecans. That is all they had to eat for two days, but within minutes they are stuffing themselves with leftovers from Doctor Tom's refrigerator.

After their parents died, Pedro and Lenita were trying to get to the United States in a small boat when pirates captured and sold them to the slaveholders. They are worried about what will happen to them after they talk to the FBI.

Doctor Tom tells them not to worry. He will do all he can to help and will sponsor them while they make applications for citizenship.

Rita tells them to sleep in one of the patient rooms with a high window and to lock the window and door before they go to bed. Pedro still has the gun he took from the guard, in case someone does break into their room.

George and Ben will sleep on cots in Rita's room. She will have a gun under her pillow—in case an outlaw comes to try and silence a witness.

After the kids go to bed, Rita and Doctor Tom hear George and Ben whispering about things that happened while Ben was gone.

Doctor Tom pulls his chair close to Rita and takes her hand. "Will you marry me now? At last, people are paying for the care they receive, and I have a little money saved." He squeezes her hand and chuckles. "We could go away for a day or two on a honeymoon."

Rita grins. "Can you give me a few days to buy a dress and put together a trousseau? I'm ready for a happy life and a real family."

He smiles. "Rita, I'd be glad to marry you if all you had to wear was the threadbare dress hanging behind the bedroom door at your farm. The one you wore the first few days you worked for me."

Her eyes widen. "That and my Sunday dress was all I had to wear."

"I know, and you were beautiful, in a faded dress too thin for patches. Rita, I've loved you from the first day we met. I was dreading trying to train a woman to work for me, but you came in like a dream and did everything right from the start—without any training. Especially when Betty came along." He takes a deep breath and pulls her hand to his lips.

"Tonight when you ran to my buggy and called me Tom, instead of Doctor Tom, and said someone was in *our* barn. I was frightened but at the same time thrilled because you referred to it as our barn."

"I want to call you Tom except when in the office with patients. As well, I want George, Ben, and everything we have to be ours—together."

"I want the same." He pulls her into his arms. Rita turns her mouth to meet Tom's lips.

The following morning, the sky is clear, with bright sunshine melting the snow. It runs off the roof in rivulets. Rita hums as she fries sausage and stirs scrambled eggs. Biscuits are browning in the oven, and coffee is perking when everyone gathers at the table.

Ben is the first to hug his mama. "You don't know how good it feels to be home, and to know I'll get to eat a good breakfast instead of the garbage they collected from restaurants in town—slop supposed to feed a farmer's pigs. They pulled a truck into the field and told us to eat what we wanted from the dirty truck bed. The first day I couldn't eat, but afterward, I grabbed half-eaten sandwiches or hands full of wilted vegetables and overripe fruit. Sometimes we could find a cookie with only one missing bite. Everyone was starving and grabbing at anything they thought wouldn't make them sick. What we didn't eat, or save in a pocket, was dumped along the road for the gators. We didn't get to eat again until the next day when another truck came in filled with more garbage."

Rita turns off the stove and puts an arm around Ben. "Son, try to let it go. You'll have to tell it all to the FBI, but for now, enjoy being home."

"It's not easy to forget. I thought I was going to die, and what stuck in my gut, was knowing my pa sold me to those devils."

"Boys, Luke is crazy. He has been for as long as I've known him. Something is missing in his brain. Most animal parents try to protect their young, but Luke only has feelings for himself. From this day forward, forget Luke and think of Tom as your dad. Tom and I will be married soon, and he wants to be a good parent for you."

George looks at the clock and stuffs his last bite of eggs into his mouth. "I need to get going. I told Mr. Smith I'd help him cull some cattle to sell. Ben, do you and Pedro want to go with me?"

Pedro nods. "I want to go. I worked on a ranch for a year. I'm good with horses and a lariat."

"Really?" George says. "I'm trying to learn how to throw a lariat. Will you teach me? I can twirl it, but I can't catch a thing."

"Sure. I'll help you."

Ben shakes his head. "I want to stay here with Mama. I think those men are still after Pedro and me. We are the ones who put those two guards on the ground. And if that Louisiana sheriff comes looking for us, don't any of you tell him a thing. One day when a different driver brought the truck with the leftover food in the back, I heard two of the boys whispering that it was the sheriff that sold them to the guards. They said they asked him for help, but he locked them in jail, and the next day turned them over to guards from the camp."

"Ben, are you sure? Rita asks.

"Yes. I wouldn't say it if I wasn't. One of those boys had a knot on his head where the sheriff hit him. It took a long time to heal and caused him bad headaches."

"I'll report that to the FBI. They are already investigating him."

George frowns. "Okay, Ben, I don't blame you for staying here, but I promised Mr. Smith I'd work today. Pedro, do you think you should stay here in the house until those men are caught?"

Pedro turns to Rita. "I will leave my rifle here with you if you will let me take the pistol. I enjoy being outside with the cattle, but I need a gun for protection."

"It's not my gun. It belongs to Doctor Tom. He left early to check on a patient and may not return until nearly noon. I think it's wise for you to stay inside this house today. The doctor has dominoes, checkers, and several books you can read to pass the time."

"I cannot read except in Spanish. Lenita can read a little English, but not well."

"I'll start teaching you. If you are going to live in this country, you need to know how to read and write the language. I have a few beginning books, and I can get more from the Public Library."

Pedro nods. "Chasing cows from the back of a horse is more fun, but I will take your advice. I need to learn English reading."

The Doctor's Luck

19 ~ Night in a Cave

The snowstorm moved east, and the afternoon sun is warm. After finding a couple of books brought in for Betty, Rita decides to go to her farm to look for books she kept for the boys when they were learning to read. Luke is in jail, so she is no longer afraid to venture away from the house, especially with Tom's gun in her jacket pocket. Pedro has a rifle for protection if strangers come around to cause trouble for the children.

She slips into a pair of old blue jeans and boots, ties a large scarf on her head, and stuffs leather gloves in a pocket with a clean white handkerchief. Rita has always loved walking and being outside. After telling the children where she is going and that she plans to return before dark, she starts down the road, walking fast.

She finds the door of her house unlocked, but nothing seems to be missing. George must have forgotten to lock the door when he left. Rita pulls a cardboard box from underneath her bed, takes six books the boys loved in their younger years, along with a book of nursery rhymes, and a copy of *Huckleberry Finn*. Placing the books on the kitchen table, she walks to the barn.

She can almost see her pa, building something with his hammer and saw, or sharpening a tool. She does not hear any chickens clucking, and there are no eggs in the hen house. The garden is bare, except for long, dead vines without peas, and a few turnips with short-cropped green leaves.

Feeling freedom, as she has not experienced for a long time, she jogs toward the creek and stands to watch water rushing past rocks and bushes near the banks. Many times she played here as a child with her mama and pa nearby. The voices of George and Ben laughing and contending while skipping rocks seem almost real, and—Luke! With a gasp, she turns and runs along the bank.

Luke's cruel voice and haunting laughter echoes after her. "Ri-ta, I came back to get you."

She could outrun Luke when she was younger. Can she still? She hasn't run much since the boys were born, but Luke was always lazy, and he has put on more weight.

Where the water flows low over small rocks and curves to the left, she dashes across and runs next to the bank beside thick woods, land Luke didn't know her pa owned, and an area where Rita is not as familiar, because she didn't want to frighten the deer living there.

Seeing a sycamore tree, blown over during a wind storm, slanting next to a high bank, Rita remembers Luke could never walk a foot-log and rushes up the trunk to where the crown tilts against a cliff. Near the top, she feels the tree shake as her weight starts it slipping toward the creek. Seconds before it rotates to go crashing into the water below, Rita grabs onto a rock protruding from the cliff. Swinging a leg over the edge, she rolls onto a flat stone and reaches to grasp a small tree trunk. Pulling herself further upon the ledge, she moves closer to the bluff.

She cannot see Luke; neither can he see her, but she hears him approaching in the dry leaves on the opposite side of the creek. Remaining still, except for her pounding heart, she is afraid to move or even breathe, but she suppresses her breath to small huffs.

How did he escape, and how can I get down from here and to town without getting killed? Someone must have told him my divorce was final, or he read it. A notice did appear in the local paper. Does he think killing me will soothe his anger?

When she hears him moving farther up the creek, she rolls to her right and notices a dark spot beyond the bush. Squinting against the sun, she realizes there is an opening in the mountain, a cave where she can seek shelter from a winter storm if another one should roll in, and protection from Luke—he can't see the opening from below.

Being careful not to make a sound, she crawls toward the gaping hole inviting her to safety. If summer were the season, she would worry about snakes, but they should be in hibernation. What about animals—a mountain lion, wolf, badger, or a skunk? Sniffing the air, she does not detect an animal scent and scoots closer. The ledge slopes toward the mouth of the cave and slants to the side, so rainwater runs off before entering the opening.

Before moving again, she listens for Luke and hears him moving still farther along the creek bank toward the west. Rising to her knees, she crawls inside the cavity and discovers a room almost ten feet across with a ceiling low enough for her to touch. A pile of dry wood leans against the wall, but she has no matches. *At least one human used this cave in the past, but who and how long ago? I hope it wasn't Luke.*

Rita walks around inside, looking up for a hole to let smoke escape. Near the back, she notices a long slender plant root hanging from the ceiling. Rita swings on it, bringing a shower of dirt and gravel down on her head. Bending low, she shakes her head and combs fingers through her long hair. *I hope there were no bugs or worms in that dirt.* Again she shakes her head and combs her hair with chilled fingers.

Before dark, I need to know if I can walk off this mountain. I climbed trees as a kid, but not boulders. Stepping from the cave, she sees Luke almost a half-mile away at the edge of the creek. The sapling she held to while climbing onto the ledge is a young persimmon tree with several bright orange orbs. This area had frost, so they should be ripe. Taking a step toward the tree, she stops at the thought of Luke seeing her picking fruit. There should be an opportune time near sunset. She eases sideways, looking toward the west edge of the rock entrance. A large cedar tree stands where the rock ends. She might climb down the thick cedar, but the rough bark and barbed branches would eat at any exposed skin. She will not try that unless other efforts fail.

Turning toward the persimmon tree, she notices the grass is worn down on a narrow path, next to the rock wall going down for approximately thirty feet and ten in the upward direction. Some animal has been coming in and going out of the cave. There are no tracks on the hard surface, *but what if she has to spend the night here and a ferocious animal returns?*

On her way into the cave, she pulls a handful of dry grass and picks up a few leaves. She has never tried to start a fire with friction but has heard stories of mountain men and Indians doing it. She finds a flat rock, not much bigger than her hand, and one that is narrow and pointed. After shredding the leaves and grass close around the flat rock with small sticks surrounding them, she puts on the leather gloves and rubs the sharp rock back and forth over the flat one until her arm and shoulder aches. She is about to give up when a tiny spark ignites a thin, dry leaf and spreads to grass and sticks. "Thank you, Lord, for answering my prayer."

The dry sticks and wood left inside the cave make very little smoke, and the lapping flames cannot be seen from below. The fire is directly under the tiny hole where she pulled down the root, but the opening is not large enough for a vent. She sits on the ground between the fire and the rear of the cave, hoping Luke cannot smell the smoke and wondering what kind of animal might creep in to join her.

Sitting beside her fire, she also wonders if Tom is home, and if he and her boys know Luke escaped from jail. What will Tom do when he discovers she left to get books from the farm and has not returned? If she builds a big fire to signal help, Luke may come for her first. She runs her hand over the cold steel of Tom's gun, tucked snug in her pocket, and asks herself, "Could I shoot Luke if he appeared in the mouth of this cave?" With a shiver, she remembers him yelling, "I came back to get you!" Rita knows he intends to kill her.

How would Ben answer her question? Or George and Tom? She doesn't wonder long about their answer, and without a doubt, she is aware of Luke's plan. She must protect herself to spare her boys and Tom from grief.

Rita sits in the cave all afternoon, trying to figure a way to escape without getting killed. A dark shadow from the cedar tree covers the front of the cave, and the western sky turns blood red before she ventures outside to pick the persimmons. Gathering all she can reach, she drops them in her cupped shirttail. Once inside, she sits beside the small fire and bites into one, almost expecting it to draw her mouth like a taste of alum, but it is ripe and sweet.

With a thumb and finger, Rita pulls a slimy brown seed the size of a large butterbean from her mouth and flings it into the fire. Repeating the process with several others, she listens as they sizzle and pop.

After eating three persimmons, she is thirsty but has no water in the cave. Sitting near the entrance, she tries to concentrate on listening for sounds of rescuers, or a predator. She hears the wind in the tops of tall sycamore trees along the creek, an owl searching the hills above her for supper, and a timber wolf howling for its mate, but water gurgling over rocks below seems the loudest.

Once more, Rita shivers. What if a timber wolf decides to come inside the cave? Or a mountain lion—a sure-footed cat would have no trouble slinking along the ledge. She walks outside. The surrounding timber, cloaked with darkness, looks frightening. Running her left hand along the rocks, she moves beyond the persimmon tree, then stops. One wrong step and she might land on the rocks thirty feet below. Easing sideways along the ledge, she goes back to add more wood to her fire and sit near the flames.

A yellow moon has risen and is shining bright when she hears dogs howling in the distance. Are they some farmer's 'coon hounds, or could they be bloodhounds searching for Luke? Maybe Tom and her boys found someone to look for her.

When Rita gets so sleepy that she can barely hold her eyes open, she drags a large log from the woodpile to the fire. It should burn all night, and maybe keep wild animals out of the cave. Luke may be able to see the light inside the cave, but surely he won't try climbing up in the dark. Leaning against the back wall, she falls asleep.

Before full daylight, Rita wakes, cold, hungry, and thirsty. Yawning, she feels her dry lips cracking, but places more wood over the small flames still flickering on the charcoal remains of last night's log. Shivering while waiting for the fire to blaze, she pops one of the persimmons in her mouth. It does little to quench her thirst, but at least it is moist and sweet.

Gathering dry leaves blown into the cave, she drops two hands full of them on the wood to accelerate the fire. Stepping back quickly as they flare, she shrieks when a slug hits the rock wall and ricochets, knocking Luke backward and causing him to fall, screaming over the cliff. His voice fades as he drops lower and lands with a thud on a pile of rocks.

Easing close to the edge, she grips the persimmon tree and looks over to see Luke spread, unmoving, upon rocks and debris left by earlier storm-water. A few feet away, a double-barrel shotgun rests on a grassy mound. That's Pa's gun! It's the reason my door was unlocked. I forgot to check and see if the shotgun was missing. I thought Luke was in jail, so I wasn't worried about a gun. He took Pa's gun to kill me, but Satan got him instead.

Rita drags most of the remaining wood to the cave's entrance and places it over a burning limb. When it is blazing high, she sits on a rock and eats the rest of her persimmons. Soon she hears shouting in the woods across the creek.

Standing, Rita can see Tom, the sheriff, and two deputies. She waves and calls, "Bring a long rope and let it down from above. The path is too narrow for me to leave without a rope to hold onto in case I slip."

Pointing toward Luke, she shouts. "The slug he meant for me ricocheted and knocked him off the cliff."

The sheriff nods. "Don't worry about him. We'll get him later."

"How are the children?" Rita asks.

"Fine. They are with the Smiths."

"Then please help me off this mountain. I think Luke is past sensing pain, but I'm hungry and very, very thirsty."

A deputy lowers a canteen of water with a rope. After Rita drinks her fill, she ties the rope around her waist, loops the canteen strap over her shoulder, and walks along the narrow trail until she exits onto a high meadow overlooking the valley.

Tom is waiting with open arms. After leading her away from the cliff, he kisses and hugs her again. "Rita, I led a dull life until you came along. Now, every day seems to bring a new drama, but I still want to marry you."

Rita chuckles and reaches to hold his hand. "And I want to be your wife, but now, let's go find some food. All I've had to eat since breakfast yesterday is a handful of persimmons."

The sheriff and his deputies set about the task of taking Luke to the undertaker. After getting books from the farmhouse, Rita and Doctor Tom leave for the Smith's home to pick up the children.

While the boys worked with the cattle, Mrs. Smith and Lenita prepared roast beef with all the trimmings. They insist Tom and Rita must join them for the noon meal. Rita, without delay, accepts the invitation.

As they eat, Mrs. Smith praises Lenita's skills. "Rita, I hope you and Doctor Tom don't mind, but I've asked Lenita if she would like to live here and work part-time for me. She can go to school and work in the evenings and on Saturday, helping me with cooking, cleaning, and laundry. She has agreed. Do you have any objections?"

"No. I think it is a good opportunity for Lenita."

Mr. Smith waves a hand in the air. "Pedro has also agreed to stay here, go to school, and help George and Ben with my farm work."

Ben turns to Rita. "Are you going to leave George and me at the farm or at Doctor Tom's while you go away on a honeymoon?"

Rita shakes her head. "I'll hire one of the ladies from town to stay with you."

Mrs. Smith gasps. "Oh. There is no need for you to hire someone. They can stay here. We have plenty of room, and the boys will be here every day helping feed the cattle. They'll be out of school on Thursday and Friday for Thanksgiving if you decide to go before then."

Tom reaches for Rita's hand. "You can go to town on Monday to buy a dress and whatever else you need. We can get married on

Tuesday and come home on Sunday. If we go to Little Rock, you can shop for other things you want while we are in the city."

"It seems strange getting married so soon after Luke died."

Mrs. Smith straightens. "Don't be foolish. For years, Luke caused you grief. Everyone around this area is proud of you and Doctor Tom. Your divorce is final, Luke left you for over two years, and he made more than one serious attempt to kill you. Get married with God's blessing."

Rita's eyes open wide. "Does anyone know how Luke escaped from jail?"

Tom swallows a mouthful of coffee. "When the deputy came into the cell to pick up the breakfast tray, Luke stabbed the deputy with his fork. He missed the man's jugular vein. Thank God, the deputy should recover without complications. Luke was nowhere in sight when the sheriff came back from breakfast and found the deputy."

"Why did Luke have a fork? I thought prisoners got spoons."

Tom nods. "That's the rule, but a teenage girl, a new employee at the restaurant, prepared his tray. No one told her to only send a spoon.

20 ~ The Wedding

Riding home in the buggy with Tom, Rita leans back, staring at him. "I bet the parents of young unmarried women in this community are angry because we are engaged."

"Why do you think that? I thought the young men must all be jealous of me."

Rita laughs. "I don't care who is jealous or angry. I love you, and I'm happy." She snuggles close to hug him.

His laughter joins hers. "It is so good to laugh and see you happy."

"It's good to be happy and know Luke can't come back to bother my boys or me again. Yesterday, I was afraid if he appeared in the cave, I wouldn't be able to shoot him. I kept praying for God's help, and He answered my prayer."

Tom wraps an arm around Rita's shoulders and pulls her closer. "Rita, on Monday morning, let's go to the courthouse in Conway and get married if we can find a minister or a justice of the peace nearby. You can wear your Sunday dress, and buy whatever else you need in Little Rock."

"I hoped to have a new dress and a beautiful silk gown before the wedding. I want to dance with my prince by candlelight in a beautiful gown, so we will remember our dance for the rest of our lives." She laughs. "It's my childhood dream."

He looks at her and grins. "Conway has several stores with pretty things for ladies. You can buy what you want, and put on the new dress before our wedding. Now is a good time for me to take a few days off. I don't have a patient expecting a baby within the next three months, and the rest of my patients seem to be doing well."

"Okay. Tomorrow, after church, I'll talk to Mrs. Smith again to make sure it's okay for the boys to stay there next week. Maybe she can give me her answer right then."

Mrs. Smith's face brightens as she grabs Rita in a tight hug and kisses her cheek. "I'm so happy for you and Doctor Tom. Of course, your boys can stay at our house next week and any time you want."

Monday morning, Tom calls all patients with appointments that have phones, gives notice to the storekeeper and sheriff, and hangs a sign on his front door, stating: "The doctor and nurse are away on a honeymoon. We will be back next week."

Word of their leaving spreads fast. Townspeople exit buildings to stand on walks and driveways, waving and calling good wishes as they drive through town on their way to Conway. Ruth Parker and her husband stand on their front porch, holding the twins. The sheriff and his deputy wait beside the police car and tap the siren for one long wail. At the school, George, Ben, Pedro, and Lenita stand by the gate, waving as the school bell rings, and small children on the playground clap their hands.

Tom and Rita wave to everyone until they reach the cemetery, where three old men with shovels are digging a grave. One man tosses his shovel out, with a loud clang, frightening a flock of crows. They rise from the surrounding trees, flapping their wings and cawing.

Rita shivers. "I wish they had sent Luke to Louisiana. I don't like him being here with our family and friends."

"I tried to get the sheriff to ask the county to send him to Louisiana, but he said shipping him there would be a big expense, and I doubt that Louisiana wants him any more than we do. At least his grave is off by itself away from everyone else. Try not to think of him."

"I'll try, but my boys have his name. Every time someone looks at his grave, they'll think of George and Ben."

"I'd be pleased for them to take my name if they want."

"I'll ask them, but it might attract more attention than they want since they've had that name all their life."

The morning is windy but excellent for traveling when snuggled under a thick blanket. Rita and Tom talk and laugh most of the way. "We'll be getting into town soon. Do you want to eat lunch before we go to the courthouse?"

"Yes, I want a chili-dog and a bowl of ice cream for dessert."

"Are you sure? I'll buy you a steak dinner if you want."

"I'm sure. I want something I don't often cook at home."

"It's your choice. There's a small café nearby. After we leave the courthouse, we'll head for Little Rock."

They both order chili-dogs and ice cream and sit enjoying the meal. At the courthouse, they fill out the paperwork while listening to people talking about a winter storm rolling in from the southwest, bringing ice and snow.

Rita is about to panic before the clerk hands Tom the marriage license and says, "If you get married here in the courthouse, you can turn the signed license in today. Otherwise, be sure to bring it in and get it registered before the deadline."

Tom looks at Rita, "Do you mind getting married now? We can shop afterward."

She looks down at her Sunday dress and pulls the skirt fabric together to hide a thin spot. "Okay. That's fine."

Tom asks the clerk, "Do you have a minister or justice of the peace here to marry us now?"

"Yes. Do you want me to send for one?"

"Please do."

The clerk calls to a young man and sends him to get a justice of the peace. Within minutes Tom and Rita are married, with the license registered. While Tom reaches for his wallet to pay, the man asks them if they plan to spend a few days in town.

Tom tells him they plan to drive on to Little Rock.

The man shakes his head. "Son, I don't think that's a wise idea. The radio says a terrible storm with sleet and snow is coming in from the southwest. It's already near Little Rock. It left ten inches of snow across some parts of Texas. You should stay here in town, or head north or east. Wherever you are when the storm hits, you'll be stuck there for days. Think it over." He walks away, shaking his head.

Rita looks at Tom with a frown. "Tom, let's go home, please. I can shop at another time."

"Are you sure? What about your dream of a beautiful gown?"

"My dream will turn into a nightmare if we get caught in a

storm. I can postpone shopping until spring if I have to. At home, you have plenty of wood for the fireplace and a cellar full of food. We fell in love while I was wearing a faded, threadbare dress—surely, it won't matter if I don't have a fancy silk gown."

"It doesn't matter to me. Making you happy is the important issue."

They rush to where the buggy is parked and climb inside. The southwestern sky is dark, and the wind stirs leaves in the street. "Rita, if I thought we had time, I'd stop at one of these shops and buy you the prettiest gown they have, but we need to run if we beat the storm."

Rita grins. "If we beat this storm, we'll have each other and a warm fire in the fireplace. Get Dolly to trot us home."

He taps the lines against Dolly, and they are off. "Rita, I want you to know I'll love you forever—and truly as much without memories of a silk gown."

Turning to look at him, she notices a wide grin and laughs as he begins to sing a silly folk song. Together, they laugh and sing as the horse trots away.

Before they reach home, snow is falling. No one is on the street and sidewalks, but the little town is beautiful with lights in the windows of the general store, the restaurant, and the barbershop.

"Rita, I am so glad you insisted on coming home. Since snow is already falling here, it must be deep between Conway and Little Rock. We would have been caught out on the road in that storm. About now, we would be freezing to death."

Tom stops at the front door. Rita takes the bags inside as he drives Dolly to the barn. When Tom comes inside after taking care of his horse, Rita has fried bacon and eggs and made biscuits and gravy. "It's not the fancy meal you were planning at the hotel restaurant, but it was quick and will serve a purpose."

"It's wonderful. I'll be here with my appetite as soon as I wash my hands."

"Take your time. The biscuits need a few more minutes to cook."

"Then, I'll build a fire in the fireplace."

After supper, they go to the doctor's room at the back of the building. Rita has never been inside his private bedroom. He keeps the door closed, and on her first day of work, he told her it was off-limits to everyone except him.

She stands in the doorway, looking at the rock fireplace with a warm fire. A large leather couch and a matching chair occupy the space in front of the hearth. One wall is covered by bookshelves loaded with books. In front of that is a long desk with a padded chair. In one corner stands a four-poster bed, its covers turned down to smooth white sheets. On a side table, a silver tray holds a bottle of wine, two stemmed glasses, and a plate of cheese, and fruit.

"Oh. You have a beautiful room."

"*We* have a beautiful room. Everything I own belongs to you."

21~ After the Storm

Snow, mixed with sleet, is still falling the following morning. Shivering, Tom pulls on a robe and goes to rekindle the fire. "Rita, stay in the warm bed until I get a fire going in the fireplace and a flame under the coffee pot." When he returns from the kitchen, he brings a box tied with a pink ribbon. "I bought this the day I went to town to see a lawyer, but at that time I couldn't give it to you."

She pulls the ribbon and opens the box. Inside is a soft, white robe with matching slippers. Sitting on the side of the bed, she slips it on and slides her feet into the slippers. "Oh, Tom, they are beautiful. How nice." She stands to hug him.

After a long kiss, he steps away. "Sit in front of the fire, and I'll bring our coffee."

Tom brings a tray with coffee, buttered toast, and jelly.

"I've never had anyone to wait on me like this. I feel like a queen."

"I like doing things for the woman I love."

"I've never been so happy in all my life. I'm glad we came home. Now, this room is our *most* special place."

"When the town discovers we're here, you may not think so. Every time we get snow and ice, people get outside and fall— breaking bones. Others stay out too long and get frostbite. I predict we'll have a full office before noon."

She smiles and lays her hand over his. "I'm here to help. Just tell me what I need to do."

The doctor was right. The storm blew in before some knew it was coming. Mr. Evers, who lives alone except for an orphan boy, tried going to the store for groceries. He slipped and fell on the ice in front of the store. The teenage boy comes knocking on the door, yelling, "Doctor, we need help."

Tom unlocks the front door. Rita can see the older man in the bed of his wagon with two strong-looking men and the boy ready to help lift him.

Motioning toward a rolled canvas, Doctor Tom says, "Men, take my stretcher to bring him inside."

The boy, his face now showing almost as much pain as the old man, calls, "Be careful. He's got a broken leg, and he hurt his hand."

Without hesitation, Doctor Tom gives instructions. "Put him on the bed, in that first room to the right of my office. I can set his leg in there and not have to move him right away."

"Rita, tell this young man how to mix the calf milk or ride with him down to the barn in Mr. Evers' wagon."

To the boy, he says, "Pull the wagon in the barn and put the horses in stalls with hay, and give hay to my horse as well. Hold to Rita's hand as you walk up the hill, so she doesn't slip."

"Yes, sir." The boy nods and turns to Rita. "You don't need to go, Miss Rita. I know how to feed a calf and give hay to the horses."

"Okay, I'll give you a pail of warm water to mix with the powdered milk."

Rita knows it will take a long time to fix the man's leg. She puts on a big pot of coffee and mixes a cinnamon cake as the men warm their hands in front of the fireplace. She pulls out a sack of dried pinto beans and puts a pot of them on the stove to cook with ham hocks, peels potatoes, and cuts them to fry, mixes a pan of cornbread, and scoots it in the oven before removing the cake.

She is setting coffee cups on the table when the sheriff drives up with the chains on his tires clanging. He tells the men he will take them home if Mr. Evers' team and wagon are going to be in Doctor Tom's barn for a while.

The boy has returned from the barn and is watching Rita hustle around the kitchen. "Sheriff, if you're in a hurry, I'll walk. Miss. Rita promised me a slice of coffee cake."

"I'm not in a hurry if she's got enough for me to have a slice."

"There's plenty. Men, grab yourselves a cup, pour your coffee, and sit around the table. I sliced the cake, so help yourselves."

The boy devours his cake and sits staring at the one remaining piece. Rita picks up the plate and slides the cake onto the boy's plate. Eat this so it won't go to waste.

He grins. "Good food doesn't go to waste around me. I sure wish Mr. Evers had taught me how to cook before he broke his leg. I can fry eggs and bacon, but I haven't tried to cook anything else."

Rita asks, "Does he have a recipe book?"

"It's old. It belonged to Mr. Evers' grandma and is smeared with grease and bits of food. I can barely read it."

"Tell me what you want to cook, and I'll write the recipes for you."

He grins and nods. "A cake like this for starters."

"I imagine Mr. Evers will have to stay here for a few days. We'll move a cot into his room so you can help him if he needs anything throughout the night. During the days, you can help with cooking. My boys are staying with the Smiths this week. Tom and I were supposed to be in Little Rock, but when we heard about a snowstorm headed this way, we came home."

"I'm glad you did. Mr. Evers was in a lot of pain before we got here. I don't think he could have made a trip to Conway in a rough wagon."

The sheriff takes the men back to the store, but the boy waits for the doctor to tell him what to do about Mr. Evers.

Doctor Tom sets the older man's leg, puts a plaster cast on it, and comes to the kitchen to talk. "Freddy, you're going to have a big job helping Mr. Evers. He doesn't need to put any weight on his broken leg for about two weeks, but he needs to move his toes and do some exercises. You'll have to help him do them. I'll loan you a bedside chair with a chamber pot in it, but for the first few days, he'll have to use a bedpan."

"I had to help my grandpa before he died. I can do it again."

Doctor Tom sits at the table, drinking a cup of coffee when someone rings the bell. Rita rushes to answer. It is Lucy Baxter. "Nurse Rita, my grandma, slipped on the ice and broke her arm. Can I bring her in and get Doctor Tom to fix it?"

"Freddy, will you help Lucy bring her grandma inside?"

"Sure, Miss Rita."

Lucy wrings her hands, and her eyes glisten with tears. "The fall made her sick. I'm not sure she can walk up the steps. She's awful weak."

Freddy takes one look at the frail little woman and tells Rita, "Get her bed ready. I'll carry her inside." The strong boy lifts her like a baby and carries her up the steps and into the bedroom.

Doctor Tom sets Grandma Baxter's arm and puts a cast on it before going into the kitchen for lunch. He asks Freddy and Lucy to join them at the table.

"Lucy, your grandma has a weak heartbeat. I want to keep her here overnight, in case she has distress. Maybe, she can go home tomorrow, but you'll need to sleep on a cot in her room tonight and help her with anything she needs."

Before the day is over, Doctor Tom has four more patients. One for croup, one for tonsillitis, one for a sprained ankle, and another broken arm. "Rita, those people would have been in trouble if we were in Little Rock, but I hate that we didn't get our honeymoon."

"We can go later. If possible, I think I love you more because you are so compassionate to needy people."

Freddy and Lucy go to feed the calf and horses while Rita prepares supper. Freddy comes inside laughing because Lucy likes the calf so much. "Lucy, have you not ever lived on a farm?"

"No. My parents lived in Kansas City, and my grandma lives here in town. I love animals. Baby calves, dogs, and horses more than any. I would like living on a farm."

"I fed Mr. Evers' animals this morning before we came to town, but I'll need to go tomorrow morning and put out more hay.

Lucy, do you want to go with me? I'll have to take the wagon."

"Yes, I want to go, if Rita doesn't need me to stay and help with grandma."

"Your grandma should be fine after she eats her breakfast. I don't mind if you go. Do either of you still attend school when we don't have snow?"

Lucy nods, "I do. I'm a senior."

Freddy shakes his head. "I'm supposed to be a senior, but I didn't have money for books and school clothes after my grandpa died, so I went to work for Mr. Evers. He's a nice man and I like working with animals and taking care of the farm. The bank took my grandpa's farm because he had a loan against it when he got sick. I wanted to take it over, but I wasn't eighteen, and they wouldn't let me."

Rita prepares a plate of food for Mr. Evers and asks Freddy to help him. He eats everything on the plate and jokes he'd forgotten how good food, cooked by a woman, could taste.

Lucy prepares a plate for her grandma and sits to feed her. Grandma eats a few bites before falling asleep. With a sad face, Lucy goes to join Rita, Doctor Tom, and Freddy. "I'm worried about Grandma. She seems to be getting weaker, even before she fell she seemed feeble. What can I do to help her get stronger?"

"Do your best to make sure she eats well and gets enough sleep. Tomorrow, I'll start her on vitamins with iron."

There is still no school on Wednesday because of accumulated snow on country roads, so Lucy goes with Freddy to feed Mr. Evers' animals. Late in the morning, George, Ben, and Pedro come to feed the baby calf. They are surprised to find Rita and Tom at the house and glad the calf didn't have to go hungry while the storm was raging.

George says, "Mama, I was afraid our calf might be dead, but Mr. Smith wouldn't let us leave during the storm, and we have to go back. Men are coming this afternoon to take away sixty head of the Smiths' cattle. He gave Ben and me five weaning calves for our work. He said we could leave them on his farm until spring and then move them to our farm. Mr. Smith is the nicest man I've ever known, except for Doctor Tom and Grandpa."

"You can stay at the Smiths if they need help with the cattle, but try to come home for Thanksgiving. We came back because of the storm. Now we have to stay until Mr. Evers and Mrs. Baxter are well enough to go home."

"Aw, Mama, I'm sorry you didn't get to go to Little Rock. Shopping in a big town would be a treat for you."

"Yes, but that is trivial compared to the pain of broken bones. Mr. Evers and Mrs. Baxter might have died from the stress of such pain before they got to Conway. I'm glad we were here so Doctor Tom could help them."

The Doctor's Luck

22 ~ Thanksgiving

Helping with Betty's twins was a joy, and Rita fought the tears after Ruth took them home. *I loved those babies, but Ruth needed them, and they need her.* Through the kitchen window, Rita watches her sons stroll toward the barn to get the horses. Her boys are growing up fast. She misses their impulsive kisses and little boy innocence, yet she is proud of the Christian men they are becoming.

On Wednesday, Rita starts baking in preparation for Thanksgiving. A farmer brought Doctor Tom two bushels of ripe apples, and another brought two sacks of sweet potatoes. He asks, "Rita, do you want to keep any of these up here, or do you want me to put them in the cellar?"

"Take one sack of sweet potatoes to the cellar. I plan to make pies for some of the needy people who prayed for Ben, and I'd like to make a few pints of apple butter. Ripe apples won't keep long before they start to rot. It would be a shame to let them ruin."

Freddy needs to go feed Mr. Evers' cattle and asks Lucy if she wants to ride along. Lucy's eyes seem to light up at his question, but her face turns pink as she asks, "Do you mind, Miss Rita? I'll peel apples and sweet potatoes when we get back. I might be in the way while you make all those pie crusts."

Rita grins. "You wouldn't be in the way, but I only have ten pie plates. When I fill those, I'll be ready to peel apples."

"Grandma has four big glass pie plates. We'll stop by and get those. She won't mind if you borrow them."

"Fine. We'll use her plates for our pies so they won't get misplaced or lost. It's a nice day for a ride, but Freddy, don't you keep her away too long. I can use a woman's help today. Oh, will you stop by the store and see if they have some empty boxes for delivering the pies?"

"Sure, Miss Rita, we can do that."

Above the noise of the rattling wagon, Rita hears the young couple laughing. She missed her teen years of courting, but shrugs, "No time to mull over the past. The Lord has blessed me."

When Lucy and Freddy return, Rita has four apple pies cooling on the counter and two big pans of cornbread baking for making cornbread dressing.

"Freddy, are you a hunter?"

"Yes, when I have time. I keep the rabbits out of our garden. Mr. Evers likes rabbit stew, and fried rabbit when I get a young one."

"Have you ever hunted geese?"

"No. I've never tried. Mr. Evers told me not to bother. He doesn't like the taste of geese. He thinks they have a fishy taste."

"I need to make some dressing, and I don't have a chicken or turkey. If you'll go over to my farm and the creek behind the house, I think you'll find a few geese still hanging around. Bring me a couple. If you see any chickens in the yard, bring those too. I'm cooking for needy families. I don't think they will complain. The dressing should taste good after I season it with onions, sage, and pepper."

Before dark, Freddy returns with three geese and two

chickens. Rita boils the chicken and geese in separate pots, adds onion, garlic, and crumbled sage leaves with the geese, and saves the broth from the chickens for making more dressing. "We don't have a turkey or young tender chickens for tomorrow, so we'll have chicken dressing with vegetables for our Thanksgiving meal."

Freddy says, "Mr. Evers has a big turkey he's been saving for today. I'll ask him if he wants me to go get it."

The old man shouts, "Yes, boy, I should have told you earlier. Get it. I've been watching that Tom grow all summer in anticipation of eating a drumstick on Thanksgiving."

"Good," Rita answers. "Freddy, will you pull off the feathers and put the dressed bird in a tub of cold water on the porch with boards over the tub so a dog can't carry it off? I don't have room in the refrigerator for a turkey and all this dressing. In the morning, I'd like for you and Lucy to deliver the pies and dressing to families on my list. Do you mind?"

"I'll be glad to deliver food to needy people, and I'm sure Lucy will like helping."

It is late before Rita finishes peeling and cooking sweet potatoes for her gift dinners. In the morning, she will mash and mix them with butter and brown sugar.

While she peels sweet potatoes, Doctor Tom pulls meat from the birds and has it chopped and ready for making the dressing in the morning. "Goodness, Rita, you sure took on a job."

"I know, but I would hate for those people who prayed for Ben to go hungry on Thanksgiving while we stuff ourselves."

The following morning, Rita is up before daylight. Tom raises on an elbow and asks, "Why are you up so early? Today's a holiday."

Rita shakes her head and chuckles. "Not for wives and mothers. I have pies, rolls, and a turkey to bake. Stay in bed while you can. It may not be a holiday for you either, but I'll call if a patient arrives."

A thin layer of ice covers the tub of water holding the turkey. Rita yanks the bird from the container, sloshing water over her shoes. Shivering, she rushes inside and flops the turkey into a roasting pan. After rubbing melted butter and salt over the bird, she places sliced onion inside, covers the pan, and puts it in the oven to bake while she mixes cornbread dressing.

After they deliver ten pies, ten pans of dressing and as many bowls of sweet potatoes, Freddy and Lucy go to feed Mr. Evers' cattle, before returning to feed George and Ben's calf and the horses.

As he steps onto the porch, Rita hears Freddy groan, "Oh, I hope we didn't give all those apple pies away. I've been hungry for a pie since I first caught the scent of apples and cinnamon."

At eleven-thirty, George and Ben ride into the barn on two of Mr. Smith's horses. The sheriff meets them near the kitchen door. Rita cannot mistake the sheriff's loud voice saying, "Last week, your mama invited me for dinner. I never forget a dinner invitation."

Tom opens the door, offers the sheriff a cup of coffee, and leads the way to his big waiting room where a fire blazes in the fireplace. Two folding tables hold plates, silverware, bowls, and platters of food.

Freddy and Lucy take plates on patient trays to Mr. Evers and

Grandma Baxter and help them while Rita and her boys take the remaining food to the covered tables.

After everyone stuffs themselves, Rita and Lucy put away the leftovers and wash the mountain of dirty dishes and pans. George and Ben get ready to leave for the Smith farm to help Pedro feed hay to the Smith's cattle.

George asks, "Mama, do you mind feeding our calf in the morning? Mr. Smith wants us to work on his fence before we turn all those weaning calves out of the lot. He asked us to stay there tonight, so we'll be ready to start tomorrow morning."

"Sure, I'll be glad to feed it. I like your little calf. I think it will make a fine cow someday. Be careful, boys." With a smile, she throws a kiss to them.

Friday morning, after everyone eats a hearty breakfast, Doctor Tom goes into his office. Freddy and Lucy go to feed Mr. Evers' cattle. Rita washes the dishes and heads toward the barn to feed the calf. She hums an old gospel song as she walks across the spongy ground where snow has melted.

Before reaching the barn, Rita hears the calf bawling and quickens her steps. Setting the bucket of water on a bench, she is reaching for the bag of powdered milk when a man's hand clamps over her mouth. He holds tight, crushing her lips against her teeth.

"Don't scream or I'll shoot. That's a gun poking your ribs. Luke promised me a hundred dollars if I'd kill you. I know he's dead, but if you want to live, give me the money. I need it to get away from this area. Remember, don't scream." He takes his hand from her mouth and steps back.

Rita starts to speak. "I don't . . . ."

"Don't make excuses. I know that doctor has money. If I have to shoot you, I'll go after those skinny boys. I've had them in my sights a dozen times or more during the past week. Now, march up to the house and get money so I can leave this place."

Rita walks slow, trying not to panic. She has a little more than one hundred dollars in the baking powder can, but she wants to see this man go to jail. She knows he will keep returning if she gives him money and lets him go.

Opening the kitchen door, she hears someone in the waiting room with the doctor. "Stand here." She whispers. "I have part of it in this pantry and part in a jar under the sink."

As he turns his head to look toward the sink, Rita grabs and slams the wood pestle for her colander against his hand. He drops the gun. With a loud bang, a bullet hits the pantry ceiling. Running from the kitchen, he leaves a bloody trail.

The sheriff and Doctor Tom rush into the kitchen.

Rita yells, "Go after him! He threatened to kill my boys."

From the porch, the sheriff shouts, "Stop, or I'll shoot!"

The man stumbles and falls. Before he can get up, the sheriff grabs him by the arm and jerks him to a standing position. "Tom, look at his hand. What did she hit him with?"

Rita walks toward them with a towel for the bleeding hand. "I hit him with the hardwood pestle for my colander. I keep it on the top shelf of the pantry, but I left the colander and pestle on a towel-covered shelf to dry after I made apple butter. He may have broken bones in his hand, along with a couple of smashed veins. I hit him as hard as I could."

After mopping up blood in the kitchen, Rita goes to the barn to mix warm water with the powdered milk. The starving baby calf is trying to reach through the fence to lick the bucket as Rita stirs to dissolve the milk powder.

While watching the hungry calf, Rita prays that no more men want to kill her.

Doctor Tom wanted to go with Rita, but with a frown, motioned for the man to follow him into a patient room. After sewing up the criminal's wound and bandaging his hand, Doctor Tom watches from a window as the sheriff leaves on his way to the Conway jail with his prisoner.

The rest of the day is busy for the doctor. Most of his patients are children, sick from playing too long in the snow.

Rita bakes several loaves of yeast bread for making sandwiches with the cold turkey, and she makes hot potato salad with the leftover mashed potatoes. Friday is another feast, with four fresh-baked apple pies.

When Rita goes to remove Mr. Evers' tray, he says, "Miss Rita, you do magic with food. I almost hate to get well. I want to stay here and eat your cooking." His leathered face brightens with a smile. "I sure hope Lucy is learning from you. I think my Freddy is falling for the girl, and I can't blame him. She's a pretty one."

The Doctor's Luck

23 ~ Wish Lists

Friday night after supper, Mr. Evers and Grandma Baxter are sleeping when Rita checks on them. Doctor Tom is reading in his bedroom. Lucy and Freddy are playing checkers in front of the fireplace in the waiting room.

"Lucy, will you make sure the doors are locked before you go to bed? Freddy, will you bank the ashes over the fireplace coals and put the screen up close, in case a spark escapes the ashes? I'm going to bed. This day has been long and tiring."

Nodding, they both answer, "Yes, Miss Rita. Goodnight."

Rita dresses for bed and returns to sit beside Tom on the couch in front of the fireplace. He puts his arm around her and pulls her close. "I know this was another rough day for you. I hope Luke doesn't have any more evil friends. That man, the sheriff took away today, was the last name on the FBI list associated with Luke."

"I'm glad the boys weren't here and glad Lucy and Freddy were gone. Who knows what could have happened if one of them had walked into the kitchen?" She sighs and leans her head against his shoulder.

"Rita, Mr. Evers, and Grandma Baxter are well enough to send home since they both have someone to stay with them and help. So, let's keep a close check on the weather, and the next time clear weather is forecast for a few days in a row, I want us to make a trip to Little Rock. Would you like that?"

"Yes. A trip to Little Rock will be nice. Do you think we can do some Christmas shopping while there? It has been a long time since I've been able to buy much more than simple food items as Christmas gifts for the boys."

"If we get to go, we'll take the opportunity to buy presents. What's on your wish list?"

She grins. "I still want a pretty gown and a new dress. My Sunday dress is almost past looking decent."

"Those were supposed to be wedding gifts. We'll buy those first. Now, tell me something you want for Christmas."

"I need a pair of dress shoes, some silk stockings, and a sweater I can wear to church when it's not cold enough for my heavy coat. I'll need to try on the shoes."

"Anything else?"

"That's enough. What do you want?"

"I want my wife to have more than one Sunday dress."

Rita looks down at her hands. "I'm not a person who needs a lot of fancy things. I don't want people thinking I'm uppity. These are hard times and there are not many women in our town who have more than one nice Sunday dress. Maybe we can buy some clothes and toys for needy children in our community."

"I like that idea. Make a list of the children and their sizes."

"Tom, you didn't say what you want for Christmas."

"I want a car, so I don't have to waste so much time trotting along in a buggy."

She sits straight and looks at him with wide eyes. "I have no idea what a car costs, but I'm sure I don't have enough money to buy one."

He laughs. "Neither do I, but I want one. If we're careful with our money for the next year, we might be able to buy one. I spent my inheritance on buying this house, but now, most of my patients are paying with cash. It doesn't hurt to dream."

She pulls a blanket over her feet and snuggles closer to Tom. "A car, how wonderful, and it wouldn't be considered a luxury for the doctor. You need one for those long trips to visit patients living out of town, and we can travel to Little Rock in less than half the time."

He laughs. "Yes, we can add a little luxury with a doctor's necessity."

Saturday morning, Freddy takes Mr. Evers home. That afternoon Tom and Lucy get Grandma Baxter into the buggy and take her home. Tom builds a fire in her fireplace and fills the wood box with firewood. Mrs. Baxter ordered a telephone installed next to her bed, so she can call for help if she needs someone while Lucy is at school. Freddy volunteered to come over every day at lunchtime and add wood to the fireplace, so Mrs. Baxter will not get cold before Lucy gets home from school.

Rita hangs a small blackboard on a nail in the kitchen with a line drawn down the middle with George and Ben's names over the sides. "Boys, this slate is for your Christmas lists."

George puts a rifle at the top of his list. Ben does the same, and both of them ask for cowboy boots and sheepskin-lined coats.

Doctor Tom looks at the lists and whistles. "Those boys are not asking for cheap gifts. Rita, do you want them to have rifles?"

"They are both dependable, but they haven't had a dad or grandpa around to go hunting with them and teach gun safety. Mr. Smith has been teaching with pistols, but I don't think with a long-range rifle. Do you have a rifle?"

"Yes, and I'll take them hunting, but one at a time. Those boys are not going to like the separation, but two boys asking questions at the same time take away from learning and can cause confusion and danger. What if I ask for a rifle as my Christmas gift? Then, I'll have two guns, one for me and another to loan one boy at a time. If they learn well, we'll buy another one later so they can each have a gun for hunting."

She nods. "You are right. They will not like the idea of hunting one at a time. They have been almost like twins since Ben learned to walk. What George does, Ben wants to do the same, but safety comes first. I like your idea."

"We'll get the boots, western hats, and sheepskin-lined coats. They need those clothes for working with cattle, and I'll check around and see if we might be able to afford a couple of horses. Didn't Mr. Evers say he has six young mares he needs to sell? Freddy rides the big gray, but I noticed two pretty black horses and a pair of red ones in his pasture. I'll ask him first. He owes me for a week's room and board, and doctor services on his leg."

"What about the pup Mr. Smith has been saving for them?"

"If they agree to take care of it and the horses, it's fine with me. Those pups are smart, like their mama. The boys will need a good cow dog."

While the boys are in school, Rita calls Mr. Smith and tells him she wants one of the pups, but does not want to pick it up until Christmas Eve.

"I sold the males, but you can have the two females. Although, I would like for you to take them now. The mama is still letting them nurse, and they're wearing her down. She's starting to look sick. I'll loan you a cage to keep them in until they get used to your barn."

Rita agrees to let the boys have them before Christmas, and tells him she'll have the boys bring the buggy to get them.

"No." Mr. Smith says, "The cage I have is big. I'll tell the boys to load it on my wagon. They can bring the wagon home after school tomorrow."

Doctor Tom sits with an empty cup and compliments Rita on her good coffee before telling her he's glad she agreed to take both of the pups.

She frowns. "They'll be good for the boys, but I hope they are not a problem in town. Two dogs may make a lot of noise."

"We have fifteen acres here. We'll keep them penned until Christmas. By then they'll be weaned and shouldn't make a lot of noise. Besides, in winter, everyone will have their windows and doors closed."

George and Ben are thrilled when Rita tells them they can have the two dogs. While waiting for the boys to come home with the puppies, Rita sits smiling, imagining Pedro helping George and Ben load the cage on the wagon, putting the pups inside, with the mama dog whining but going to her bed when told to do so. The poor mama will miss her babies.

Watching through the window, Rita slips into a coat and rushes down to the barn when she sees the wagon approaching. She is as excited as a kid to see the pups. She knows Mr. Smith's horses will need hay as well as Dolly, so she climbs into the barn loft to toss down hay for the horses and sits as the boys lift the crate from the wagon and set it in the barn.

24 ~ Gifts for the Needy

After unloading the dog crate in the barn, the boys water the pups and sit to play with them. Rita tells the boys, "Go on, talk to your dogs, and feed them while I get grain for the horses." Inside Dolly's stall, Rita is petting the gentle mare when she hears a man's gruff voice tell the boys to put the dogs in the crate.

Between the boards of the stall, with the dim lantern light, Rita sees Ben open the crate, push his pup inside, and step back. George holds his squirming puppy under its belly and steps toward the cage. Ben, standing behind him, slips the pistol from his brother's pocket and fires at the man in the lamplight.

The man swears and reaches for the gun he dropped when the bullet hit his leg. Ben fires again, barely missing his hand. "Reach for it again, and I'll kill you." His speech does not quiver; the words are bold and exhibit authority—not the idle talk of a boy.

With one long leap, the outlaw vanishes into the darkness—a dotted line of blood follows him. Ben stands with the gun pointed in the direction of the man's departure, but he does not try to follow. "The world would be a better place if I had killed him. He was one of the meanest guards on that slave farm."

Rita shudders, realizing her youngest son is a man. Time spent on the Louisiana farm hardened him. She will never again see him step behind her when danger threatens.

Tom calls the sheriff before leaving the house, but seconds later, he appears in the barn with a rifle in his hand.

Rita sits on one end of Dolly's feed trough, her head against a board separating the stalls. Breathing is the only sound she makes, but her body shakes with silent sobs. Dolly continues to eat her grain, pausing once to nuzzle Rita's shoulder.

Tom runs to her. "Rita, are you hurt?"

"I didn't have a gun. I couldn't do anything to help my boys. I didn't even have the pitchfork. I left it in the loft."

He wraps his arms around her. "You did the right thing by staying in Dolly's stall. If you had run out, you might have distracted Ben and George, and perhaps given that man a chance to grab his gun."

The sheriff arrives with a deputy. They see the blood trail and follow it to Main Street, where the man must have climbed into a car. Ben saw the man at the farm in Louisiana, but he does not know his name or much information on him.

The sheriff calls the FBI. The following day two officers come to the barn. They make molds of footprints in the mud outside and write down Ben's description of the outlaw. "Son, tell us every bit of information you remember. We want to catch that guy."

He had on a baseball cap, but Ben remembers his hair was a reddish-brown when he saw him in Louisiana, and he had a bad scar on the top of his left hand.

The sheriff calls every doctor and hospital within fifty miles and asks them to notify him if anyone with a bullet wound on his leg and a scar on his left hand comes in asking for treatment.

Rita wants to keep the boys home and inside the house, but the sheriff says he thinks the man has left the state, or they would have heard something about an injured man. He suggests the boys go to school the following day, but they should not mention the stranger. "I don't want to panic this town's people into carrying guns everywhere they go."

The boys do not mention the incident at school, but as soon as they arrive at the Smith's, they tell Pedro, Lenita, and Mr. and Mrs. Smith. Pedro remembers the man and that the other guards called him Carrizo. He said Carrizo told the other guards he was from Carrizo Springs, Texas. He got stuck with his nickname while working on a cattle ranch.

Rita passes the information Pedro remembers to the FBI. Within a week, the FBI finds Carrizo in a hospital in Texarkana, Arkansas. His leg is infected. Before the infection travels to his heart, he gives detectives information on the other men who helped capture kids used as slaves on the Louisiana farm.

An FBI detective tells Rita they are on the trail of the remaining outlaws involved with the kidnapping case. All of them are in southern Texas and expected to attempt crossing the border into Mexico. The Mexican authorities are cooperating in trying to capture the men. He doesn't think they will ever try to move back into the United States.

Rita has hope, but it is hard not to fear that one of Luke's relatives could be lurking in the shadows waiting to kill her or her boys in an attempt to even a score for Luke.

Tom asks the minister, and Rita asks the owner of the general store if they know of any families in dire need of food and clothing. Members of the church are putting together food baskets for each household and one toy for each of the needy children, but no one is providing warm clothing and shoes.

Rita makes a list of the names, addresses, and the names and ages of the children. She goes to visit each house on her list, taking two apple cakes as introductory gifts and sits to visit a few minutes with the mother at each home. Before leaving, Rita knows what each child needs and the sizes. She also makes a note if the mother needs shoes or a sweater.

After supper, she sits in front of the fireplace, telling Tom about the homes she visited. "I wanted to cry as I left some of those houses. Several were just one room with boards nailed over most of the windows. One woman had to lift the door and push it in place with a chair against it to keep it from falling. She didn't have a husband. With tears in her eyes, she said her man didn't have money for a ticket and tried to hop on a moving train to go looking for a job. He fell and was killed. Do you think we could go over there on Saturday and fix the door and replace some windows?"

"Yes, but you'll need to go measure the windows so we can bring the right size."

"I'll do it tomorrow. Tom, it will take more money than I have to buy those children the essentials they need."

"I'm not going to have much left after I buy those horses for the boys."

"Maybe we shouldn't buy them this year."

"I've already made a deal with Mr. Evers. I can't renege on my word."

"Buy me one dress. I don't need the other things. My shoes are a little worn, but some of those kids and their mothers are almost barefoot. It will please me to see them happy and warm."

"I'll ask the sheriff if he can squeeze some money from a few of this town's rich old skinflints. If you make out a list of what the children need and the sizes, we'll ask the storekeeper if he will let us buy the gifts at his cost. I'm sure he'll, at least, give a discount."

Before the next winter storm, Doctor Tom and Rita replace every broken window and repair three doors at the homes Rita visited. With a good discount from the storekeeper, they buy the items on Rita's list, wrap the presents, and print names on each one.

George and Ben tell the Smiths about the gifts. Mr. and Mrs. Smith buy socks for every person on the list and fill the stockings with candy. Also, they buy toys for the children and donate a smoked ham for each family.

On Christmas Eve, Rita, Doctor Tom, Mr. and Mrs. Smith, and the sheriff deliver the gifts to the homes and return to Tom and Rita's house. Rita turns on a burner under the coffee and cuts a big chocolate cake. "I love helping people, in particular children. They all seemed so grateful for the presents."

Mrs. Smith smiles, "Remember the little red-haired girl when she put on her new shoes? She was so proud of them. She danced and twirled, and her brother was just as proud of his boots. He said, 'Now I can walk to school, and my feet won't freeze.'"

Mr. Smith sets his cup on the table. "Rita, your boys tell me you have a lot of deer in the wooded area across from your farm. Didn't your pa buy that land?"

"Yes, but I never told Luke about it. He wanted to kill the deer."

"Your boys said they saw seven big bucks at the edge of the creek in September. You don't need so many bucks with a small herd of doe. Those families could use some deer meat. I've been teaching both of your boys gun safety—with pistols and a rifle. If they killed half of those bucks and left the doe, the herd should do better. Too many bucks will start fighting and kill or injure each other."

"I don't know about letting boys go hunting with rifles."

"Tom could go with them, one at a time. They need to learn. My pa took me hunting when I was younger than your boys." He pats Mrs. Smith's hand. "Many times in the first years of our marriage, a buck deer helped to feed us through the winter. There are a lot of kids I wouldn't want to turn loose with a hunting gun, but your boys are cautious. They listen well and follow directions."

Rita frowns. "What do you think, Tom?"

"I think he's right. Boys need to learn. Those bucks need to be thinned out, and those women need the meat to feed their kids."

"Well, when you find time to go hunting, I don't have any objections."

Stomping his feet on the porch, Ben comes rushing through the kitchen. George pauses to wipe his feet on a rug at the door. "The sky's spitting small flakes of snow, and it sure is cold. Mr. Smith, we got all those calves in the corral and fed them hay. Two were bedded down in a thicket on the west side of the pasture. They were well hidden, but we had your collie with us. She found them and got them moving. I hope her pups are good cattle dogs like their mama."

"I think they will be, son. They are both smart pups."

The Doctor's Luck

25 ~ Christmas

On Christmas morning, George and Ben rush to the doctor's big waiting room where the night before they hung long wool socks from the fireplace mantle. They grab boxes from under the small decorated Christmas tree and rip open the lids. Rita notices that the socks are the last to be touched, but often, in years past, a stocking of candy and fruit was all she could give.

They set the hats on their heads. Next, they pull on the boots and sheepskin-lined coats, walk around the room, and go to look at themselves in a full-length mirror at the end of the hall. At last, they lift the stockings. George looks around and whispers to Ben, "I don't see any rifles."

"Yeah, I looked for them first. We can ask again for our birthdays or next Christmas. They spent a lot of money on needy families."

When the boys are ready to feed the calf, Rita takes an apple from a fruit bowl on the counter. Dolly can have an apple for Christmas breakfast. "Tom, do you want to walk with us this morning and feed your mare?"

"Sure, I'll walk down with you." He slips into a heavy jacket. After the boys step outside, he stuffs apples into both pockets.

The morning is crisp, with no breeze. Any snowflakes surviving last night's wind are invisible under the heavy frost.

Tom takes Rita's hand, and they hurry to catch up with the boys before they enter the barn.

George sits the bucket of warm water for the calf milk on a bench. "Why is Dolly, and Mr. Smith's horses making so much noise?"

Both boys rush down the short hall. They stand with their eyes wide and mouths gaping. "Who owns these black horses?" Ben asks.

Tom replies, "They're for you and George. They look alike, except one has four white stockings, and one has three. You can pick new names, or call them by the names they know. The man who trained them is brilliant, but he has a speech problem. Instead of Three and Four, he called them Tree and Foe."

Tom takes an apple from his pocket, cuts it in half, and asks, "Tree, do you want an apple?" The mare with three stockings nods her head. He gives her half of the apple.

Ben asks, "Foe, do you want an apple?" The four stocking mare nods her head. Tom hands Ben the other apple half."

Ben says, "I want Foe."

George grins. "Okay, Tree is mine."

Tom splits another apple and hands the halves to the boys for Mr. Smith's horses. He takes the apple from Rita's pocket, cuts it, and gives both halves to Dolly.

"Boys," Rita calls. "There are two black saddles with red blankets in the tack room." She drops her voice to a whisper as they walk near. "Don't forget your manners. The horses were Tom's idea."

George turns and wraps his arms around Tom. "Thank you. I like the Christmas gifts, the horses above all, but you are the best gift we've received this year?"

Swallowing a lump in his throat, Tom nods, "Thanks."

Ben steps close and wraps his arms around Tom. "Thanks, Dad, for everything, most of all, for loving and taking care of our mama."

Rita notices Tom's eyes glisten with emotion. Smiling and happy, she goes to mix the milk and feed the baby calf while the boys saddle the horses.

Leading his horse from the barn, George stops beside Rita. "Mama, thanks for everything. This Christmas is the best, but we still have to go feed Mr. Smith's cattle."

"I know, son. Work is a farmer's life. Every day of the year, animals need care. Since we had such a big breakfast, we won't need much lunch, but I'll try to have dinner ready by four. Can you and Ben be home by then?"

"We will unless some emergency comes up. I noticed the pecan pie. We'll do our best to be here by four."

With the empty calf bucket in one hand, Rita holds hands with Tom to walk up the hill to the house.

Inside the warm kitchen, a ham is baking. Rita pulls off her coat and hangs it on the rack before setting the coffee pot on a burner. Tom, we have two slices of chocolate cake left. Do you want one with your coffee?"

"Yes, I do. That was a delicious cake."

Rita stands beside the table and slides the cake slices onto two plates. "Tom, I'm going to cut down on baking so many cookies and desserts. I don't want to gain a lot of weight."

He frowns and stares at her. "You are not getting fat. I bet you don't weigh an ounce more than you did last summer."

Rita smiles. "Tom, I'm sure we're going to have a baby in late July or August, so I'll gain weight fast."

Tom jumps to his feet and takes her into his arms. "Oh, Rita. I was hoping for babies. I love children. I would have loved Betty's twins, but Ruth needed them much worse. Today is the most wonderful Christmas, but now I'm eager for summer when I can hold our baby."

She laughs. "Do you think the store will let me exchange my new dress for maternity clothes?"

He chuckles. "You can wear it a few times before you need big smocks, and you can wear it after the baby comes."

"If I don't get too fat."

"Rita, when I discovered Betty's dad had abandoned her in my yard, I thought it was the worst luck anyone could have, but now I know she was a blessing. The first girl who came asking about a housekeeping job frightened me. She was a spoiled child, high on her own ambitions. I shuddered at the thought of having to listen to her brag every day, but soon afterward, you and your boys came along, and I knew that you were the blessing I had been praying for. God is good, every day, all the time. He knows what we need."

Rubbing her flat stomach, she smiles. "Yes. God has been very good to me. Satan may give us problems, but God answers prayers and sends us the blessings we need."

Later that afternoon, George and Ben come bounding in the

back door. Dinner is ready except for mashing the potatoes and browning the rolls. George washes his hands and digs the potato masher from a drawer. "I'll mash the potatoes. Mama, will you put in the salt, butter, and milk? Ben, stick those rolls in the oven and set the table. I'm half-starved."

Rita measures salt in the palm of one hand and dumps it, along with a lump of butter and a splash of milk, over the drained potatoes as she listens to the happy voices of her boys.

"Mama, we rode all over Mr. Smith's farm. He gave Pedro the big red horse I've been riding, and the silver-gray to Lenita. We all rode this afternoon. Lenita rides as well as any of us. I think the Smiths have adopted Pedro and Lenita."

Rita nods. "The Smiths were lonesome without children, and Pedro and Lenita need parents."

"Yeah." Ben says, "I guess we'll all help with bailing hay next summer. Lenita can drive the team with the wagon while we load the hay. Pedro can do the cutting."

Within minutes, they are sitting at the table for Christmas dinner. Tom looks around the table with a big smile. "Boys, Rita, and I want to tell you that this time next year, you should have a little brother or sister. It ought to be born in late July or near the first of August."

Ben grins. "There's a problem. We'll need a bigger table with more space—because babies like to throw food."

George says, "I hope it's a girl. I don't think I can put up with another brother like Ben."

Ben laughs. "Buddy, you don't know how lucky you are to have a brother like me. A little sister will hang onto your leg, want you to carry her on your back, she'll pull your hair, and . . ." He lowers his voice and leans close to George. "And she'll want to go with you when you go to see your girlfriend."

George frowns at him before bowing his head while Tom asks for God's blessings, but as soon as Tom says amen, George continues to banter with Ben. "I'll make a tomboy out of a little sister. I'll teach her to ride horses and rope the calves."

Ben slaps George on the shoulder. "Okay, I can help with teaching, if she doesn't bite and pull my hair, but I think I'd rather have a little brother."

Getting up for a bowl of butter, Rita pauses to look from the kitchen window at the rope swing swaying in the cold winter wind. "I can't look at that old swing without thinking of Betty. I was working on a new rag doll for her Christmas. I embroidered the face before she died." After dabbing at a wet spot on her cheek, Rita continues, "I'm sure Betty is happy in heaven. God knows we loved her, but her tantrums would be difficult to deal with along with a new baby. God's wisdom is always the best."

Tom pauses and lays a fork on his plate. "You can finish it for our baby. It will be a nice playmate for a little girl or boy, and we can call the doll Betty Ann."

"That is a good idea. I'll do that. I don't want us to forget Betty Ann. She was sent to us for a reason."

Ben places his fork on the table and looks up at Rita. "Mama, I used to think it was funny when you would say that something terrible was sent to us for a reason, but I don't believe that anymore. I credit God with putting Pedro and me in that work camp to help all those boys escape. I'm not trying to make myself look important, but without us, I'm sure some of them would have died there. Several boys were getting too sick and weak to work or fight, and all of them were so afraid of the guards and the gators that they wouldn't dare try to fight. When that guard put his hand on Lenita, Pedro hit him with his blade, and I struck the other guard with mine as he raised his gun to shoot Pedro."

Rita smiles. "I believe you, Ben. God knows who has the faith and courage to fight for what's right."

The Doctor's Luck

26 ~ A Blue Eyed Girl

On the first afternoon following the Christmas break, George stops in the kitchen after school to hug Rita. "Mama, Bobby Omak is dead, and the sheriff took his dad to jail." He nods at Rita's gasp. "His sister told me. It happened last evening at their farm."

"Oh, my goodness, and she came to school after that." Rita plops into a chair, drying her hands on a dishcloth.

George shrugs, "Yep. Rosie said, the Sheriff knocked on the door, grabbed her pa, and was putting handcuffs on him when Bobby came out of the bedroom with a rifle in his hand. The sheriff told him to drop the gun, but Bobby lifted it to aim. The Sheriff ducked toward the floor while pulling his gun, and he shot Bobby. The bullet must have hit his heart. She said he fell and didn't move—he was dead in an instant. The sheriff took him along with Mr. Omak to Conway."

"Why was the Sheriff taking Bobby's Pa?"

"I don't know, but Rosie said her mama thought it should have been him that died instead of Bobby."

"What a sad situation."

"Rosie didn't seem upset. In fact, she said, 'Bobby and Pa were mean to Mama and me.' She lifted her head with a half-smile and said, 'I'm glad they're gone. Pa was always getting drunk and hitting Mama. I was afraid he would kill her. Most of the time, I could stay out of Pa's sight, but Bobby always seemed to find and beat on me for no other reason than to see me hurting.'"

"What do you think they will do now?"

"She said, as soon as they can sell the farm and equipment, they'll go to Missouri and live with her grandparents."

George lifts a cookie from the hot pan. "It's sad to say, but Rosie and her mama will be better off without Bobby and her pa. Rosie always seemed nice, and she was looking forward to going to church with her grandma and grandpa. She said her pa wouldn't allow her to go to church."

Ben comes in the door and rushes to get a cookie. "George, get your work clothes on. Mr. Smith has work planned for us, and we have to feed our calves."

While the boys are gone. Tom's last patient leaves, and he comes to the kitchen to sit with Rita. Before he can pull out a chair, someone knocks on the door.

"Hello, Sheriff. Come in and have a seat. I'll see if Rita will make us a fresh pot of coffee."

"Thanks, Doc, but I can't stay. I just came by to tell you that we arrested Pete Omak last night, and in the process, his son pulled a gun on me. I shot him, and now he's in the morgue. The feds have evidence that Pete was cooperating with those men holding boys in that Louisiana work camp. He was responsible for capturing and sending several boys down there."

Tom nods. "Rita thought he might be the one feeding them information."

"Most all of the kids were runaways or kids from underprivileged homes where they didn't have the finances to hire private investigators or offer money for rewards. The boys that escaped said several had died there, but they didn't know what the guards did with them—they were afraid the boys were thrown to the alligators."

"I wouldn't doubt that."

"The FBI arrested that Louisiana Sheriff. There are plenty of witnesses now that the FBI is taking a strong stand. You need to decide if you want your part of it to go public. It could turn into a nightmare when the papers start sending reporters. You may not be able to keep your part of it quiet, but you can try by asking the Feds to keep your family's name out of it.

"Mrs. Omak said she'll sell that farm and all the farm equipment. I think most of the stuff came from Rita's farm. I saw her pa's name scratched on several things. Pete Omak may have stolen it or got it as a gambling debt payment from Luke."

"Rita told me that all of her pa's farming equipment disappeared, and she thinks that Pete got most of it."

"Tell her to write down the descriptions of it, and we'll list it as stolen, and present it to the judge."

"It was definitely taken without Rita's knowledge, but she has a kind heart. I doubt she'll want to take it away from a woman that's lost her son and her husband."

The sheriff nods and turns toward the door. "I wanted to let you know, so you could think about it. Rita has a right to take back what belonged to her. Pete Omak knew it didn't belong to Luke."

Tom was right, Rita said it would almost be putting one sin on top of another to take the property from a woman and child that has no other support.

The Saturday, an auction is scheduled for the Omak farm. Tom, Rita, George, and Ben arrive early to walk around the farm equipment. Mr. Smith and his wife pull their buggy onto the yard beside Tom's. Only two other wagons are there. "Tom, why do you think there are so few people here?"

"Very few people have money to spend because of the Depression." He Whispers in Rita's ear, "Most of them know that Pete didn't take care of anything. All of this probably needs greased, oiled, and repaired."

Rita looks around and agrees. Everything is sitting outside in knee-high grass and weeds, and it is all rusted.

The time for the auction to start has passed. Tom and Mr. Smith stand watching, but only two other men have arrived. One of them shakes his head with a frown, gets in his wagon, and leaves.

The auctioneer steps upon a sturdy wooden box and begins. He starts with a low price on the mowing machine, but no one bids. He lowers it by five dollars, and Mr. Smith raises his hand.

Before the auction is over, Mr. Smith has bought a hay rake, a breaking plow, a harrow, a wagon with a hay frame, and the mowing machine. I don't reckon I need any of this stuff, but it's awful aggravating to have a piece of equipment break down when you're trying to get your hay in the barn before a rain. If you don't mind, I'll park it in Rita's barn. The boys can use it any time they want, and if the need arises, it will be close at hand."

The auctioneer tries to sell the farm, but no one will raise a hand to the bid he suggests. After calling it several times, he asks, "Does anyone want to offer a bid?"

"Mr. Smith raises a hand and offers a bid of less than half of what a good farm should bring, but Pete's land is covered with weeds, thistles, and bushes. It will need a lot of work to make it into a beautiful and workable farm.

After several tries to raise the bid, the auctioneer says 'sold' to Mr. Smith.

Most of the household items are in bad shape, but Rita buys a churn and a large crock. Mrs. Smith buys a Dutch oven and two kerosene lamps.

Mr. Smith tells George, Ben, and Pedro that if they clean the brush and thistles off the farm he bought, he will tell his lawyer to put their names in his will to get the farm when he dies. Also, they can sell hay from the fields, and walnuts and pecans from trees in the yard.

Every morning before school, George, Ben, and Pedro are up early to feed calves. After school and on Saturday, they work until almost dark cutting bushes and digging up thistles from the hayfield with an ax and grubbing hoes. On rainy days they oil and grease the equipment and have it ready by June when the days are hot and dry for cutting hay.

The boys cut and store Mr. Smith's hay in his barn before starting on the new farm. One day Mr. and Mrs. Smith drive over to look at what the boys have accomplished. The hayfield is smooth with no bushes or thistles, and the yard is cut low under the nut trees. It is another dry year, and several men have asked about buying hay from the many haystacks the boys have set up in the fields.

Tom and Rita sit on the porch one afternoon watching the mocking bird feeding her young, and squirrels gathering acorns. Rita looks at Tom with a smile. "God has richly blessed us. In a couple of weeks, we should be holding our new baby. George and Ben have grown taller and muscled within the last year. They have the ambition to be cattle farmers, and I'm confident they will be successful."

Tom takes Rita's hand and embraces it. "Yes, what we have is not luck. We are truly blessed."

A week later, Rita's labor pains begin. At ten, on Friday morning, a little blue-eyed girl is born. Tom and Rita name her Rita Ann, but they plan to call her Annie.

George and Ben rush in from the hayfield at noon and take a bath so they can hold her. Ben says, "We have to go back and haul more hay, but we don't want little Annie to start coughing and sneezing because of this hay dust."

Rita smiles, "You two will be good brothers for this girl."

Ben leaves the room, saying, "I need a drink of water. It was so hot and dry in that field this morning, and we didn't want to waste time stopping."

George watches as Ben leaves. Kneeling to touch Annie's tiny hand, he says, "Mama, we're studying about baptism in our Sunday class, and we've been reading about it in our Bibles. We want to get baptized the first Sunday that you feel like going and taking Annie to church."

"Oh, George, I am so happy. I think I will be able to go on Sunday. Tom can take care of Annie, or one of the women in the nursery will hold her. I'm proud of you for helping Ben learn about Jesus and God."

George has a somber look on his face as he shakes his head. "It wasn't me. Since Ben came home from that slave camp, he's been reading the Bible and asking lots of questions in class. He wants to learn all he can so he can teach other kids. He told me that at the camp, some of the boys never heard of Jesus, and most of what they knew of God was curse words. Ben has really changed."

"I've noticed. I'm proud of you both. God had a purpose in letting Ben go to that camp." She pauses to clear her throat. If it had been my choice, I don't think I could have let him go."

Shaking his head, George says, "Neither could I. I prayed day and night for him, and I'm sure God answered our prayers."

Annie kicks her blanket and sucks on her hand, making George smile.

"Rosie told me that the reason Bobby wanted me to meet with him was so his pa could capture and take me to that camp."

"Oh, George, I thank God that all of our prayers saved you and Ben."

The Doctor's Luck